SHO...

SOMERSE...

OF THE NINETE... ...ENTURY

CW00420847

SHOCKING
SOMERSET MURDERS

OF THE NINETEENTH CENTURY

and Other Stories of Violent or Suspicious Death

JACK W. SWEET

To Audrey
With best wishes
Jack Sweet
10/4/98

Somerset Books

in association with the

SOUTH SOMERSET MUSEUM SERVICE

First published in Great Britain in 1997

British Library Cataloguing in Publication Data

A CIP record for this book is available from the British Library

ISBN 1 861834 10 0

SOMERSET BOOKS
Halsgrove House
Lower Moor Way
Tiverton EX16 6SS
Tel: 01884 243242
Fax: 01884 243325

Printed in Great Britain by Bookcraft (Bath) Ltd

CONTENTS

Acknowledgements 7

Introduction 8

Killed for a Piece of Bacon 9

'Nothing Has Ever Been Administered to Her in Her Food' 13

The Devil of Deadman's Post 18

The Untimely End of Constable Penny 22

The Killing of Dandy Joe 29

Who Killed Mr Stuckey? 33

'How Your Hand do Shake, George' 44

'Ye Thoughtless Youths a Warning Take' 51

'What a Fool I've Been – I've Not Done it Yet' 53

The Killing in the Clover Field 58

The Slaying on Sandpit Hill 62

Suffer the Little Children 68

When Death Rode the Skimmington 77

The Fight at the Running Horse 82

The Extraordinary Case of Infanticide at Crewkerne 87

Who Cruelly Murdered Poor Betty Trump? 98

'I am Free and Innocent of the Crime!' 110

'That Fisher's Mad!' 131

The Withypool Poisoner 139

The Malignant Shooting of Joseph Dunford 146

A Jealousy as Cruel as the Grave 152

Mrs Adlam Kills her Husband 162

'It Shall be a Life for a Life Before I Sleep' 166

Jacob Wilkins Goes a-Courting – for the Last Time 171

Who Cut the Rope? – The Radstock Pit Disaster 175

The Shooting of John Dyer at The Bell 180

As flies to wanton boys are we to th' gods –
They kill us for their sport

> William Shakespeare
> *King Lear*, iv: 1

ACKNOWLEDGEMENTS

My thanks to Mr L.W. Hoskins of Tatworth, Mrs J.M. Holland of Rimpton, the staff of the Somerset Record Office, David Bromwich and staff of the Somerset Studies Library, Marion Barnes and the staff of the Museum of South Somerset, and Robin Ansell, Reference Librarian, Yeovil Library, for their help and guidance in preparing this book.

To the publishers of the *Somerset Magazine* and the *Visitor* for permission to reproduce articles acknowledged in the Sources.

To the Chard History Group for allowing me to quote from *Chard in 1851* and for permission to publish extracts from the *Diary of Arthur Hull*. Somerset Record Office hold the original manuscript on loan from the Group.

Permission to publish extracts from the *Diary of Benjamin Hebditch* was kindly given by Mrs K. Lewis and Ms E.M. Hebditch.

PHOTOGRAPHS

Copyright of all photographs belongs to the author unless shown below.
2, 12, 14, 24, Museum of South Somerset; 10, Richard Duckworth collection; 13, Somerset Studies Library; 16, the Tite collection, Somerset Archaeological and Natural History Society; 17, Chard Museum; 18, The *Westonian*; 19, photograph by Robert Gillo, SANHS; 20, the Pigott collection, SANHS; 22, Somerset Studies Library, neg. 450; 25, Radstock, Midsomer Norton and District Museum; 26, Somerset Studies Library, (0577991).

INTRODUCTION

In 1881, R.N. Worth, F.G.S., wrote in his *Tourist's Guide to Somersetshire – Rail and Road*, that in this 'pleasant' county there was '... little that was grand, but much that is beautiful'. There were 'rich meadows where cattle graze knee deep in grass, wide vales, barren rolling hills, wide table-lands crested with the richest foliage, broken by valleys in which comfortable farmhouses nestle snugly amidst orchards which in spring burst into veritable seas of blossom. For scenes of loveliness Somerset may challenge any county in England'

Four decades later, Mrs A. C. Osborne Hann in the Prologue to her book *Somerset* invited readers to 'come and wander with me through Somerset, the land of Legend, Beauty and Romance. You will find there heart's content, serenity of soul, and the satisfaction of every sense. For Somerset is utterly and supremely beautiful at every moment of the day and night, at every season of the changing year. Step lightly, gently ye who would come with me and together we will wander in the woods, through the tiny rambling villages, and the little coombes hidden in the hills. Together we will explore the townships of the West, so full of history and romance, of chivalry and pageantry, till coming at last to the mountain-tops we catch a glimpse of the Vision Splendid and fall on our knees before the revelation of the Beauty which is God.'

But, sudden and violent death stalked the townships and villages of this Vision, and the stories which follow take a glimpse into the darkness which lurked over a century ago in the land of Legend, Beauty and Romance – the Land of Summer.

KILLED FOR
A PIECE OF BACON

After putting her seven-year-old son to bed, Ruth Butcher left her cottage at North Perrott, near Crewkerne, some time after 7.30 pm on Monday, 16 March, 1874; she returned the following morning battered and dead lying on two boards in the back of a farm waggon.

At about 9.15 am on Tuesday, dairyman Eli Symes drove farmer Rendall's cows into a field at Trendlewell Lane and was puzzled by the animals' disturbed state near the small pond surrounded by bushes just inside the gate. On investigation, Eli discovered to his horror the body of a woman lying on her back at the edge of the pond with her clothes in disarray and her head under the water, wedged between two fallen tree trunks. Nearby was a large blood stained stone and blood was spattered all around.

Police Constable Joseph Williams was summoned from Crewkerne to the scene and immediately searched for clues as well as taking steps to ensure that any obvious evidence was not disturbed before his superiors could examine the area.

Constable Williams found two places in the nearby lane where there were signs of a violent struggle. Blood was on the grass banks and the hedges and there was evidence that the woman, who had not yet been identified, had been dragged some 70 yards to the pond. A man's footprints were also observed and the marks of a male knee, clad in corduroy, were imprinted in the roadside mud as well as on the clothing of the corpse. A woman's bonnet was also found in the lane, partly burnt, as if it had been used as a light to hunt for a lost object such as the murder weapon.

Leaving three villagers to guard the spot, Joseph Williams hastened back to Crewkerne where he telegraphed a report to his sergeant who was in Bristol on duty at the Races. He also called on Dr Wills and Dr Cox who returned with him to the scene of the crime.

The body was removed from the pond and Dr Wills washed the battered and bloody face. Constable Williams immediately identified the dead woman as Ruth Butcher, a single woman in her early forties who lived with her seven year-old son, John, in North Perrott where she eked out a meagre living as a weaver for Messrs Matthews and Son, Hairseating and Web Manufacturers of Crewkerne and by taking in washing. Ruth also had a fourteen-year-old daughter,

Annie, who had gone into service at Halstock a few weeks before.

Dr Cox searched the corpse and found in a pocket of her skirt, a piece of bacon wrapped in paper and tied up with jute yarn, the type used in Web factories. A farm waggon was called up and Ruth Butcher's body was gently placed on two boards and lifted into it for her journey home. Back at her humble cottage, two village women washed the body and an autopsy was carried out by Dr Cox. The injuries to the head were severe and extensive and had been inflicted by a sharp weapon and a heavy stone. However, apart from a bruise on one of the deceased's arms, there were no other signs of violence, and neither was there any evidence of sexual attack.

The case caused a sensation amongst the villagers, described by a local newspaper as 'mostly simple minded agriculturalists', and was placed in the hands of the Chief Constable, Mr Goold, assisted by Superintendent Everitt of Ilminster, Superintendent Smith of Yeovil and Sergeant Giles of Crewkerne. A reward of £100 was offered for the successful prosecution of the murderer and a free pardon would be granted to any accomplice who turned Queen's Evidence.

The police carried out a detailed search of the immediate vicinity but no weapon or other clues were found. However, a trail of blood-stains was discovered on gates and stiles across fields towards Hardington, then back to Haselbury where the clues finally ended in Danes Field not far from the Vicarage.

The inquest opened before the Coroner, J. Wybrants Esq., with the Reverend Mr Down as foreman of the jury, in two rooms at Mr Slade's farmhouse on Thursday 19 March. Mr Slade also 'provided refreshments in the most liberal manner'.

Evidence was given by neighbour, Margaret Poole, who stated that she had visited Ruth Butcher at about half past five on the fatal evening and found her complaining of feeling poorly with pains in her head and chest. Another neighbour, James Marks, had heard Ruth talking to her son at about 7.15 pm and the cottage door close between 7.30 and 8.00 p.m.. A woman's scream was heard sometime after 10.15 pm by a villager who lived near Trendlewell Lane. Eli Symes provided evidence of the finding of the body and details of the post mortem were given by Dr Cox who commented that apart from the savage injuries and signs of pleurisy in one of her lungs, Ruth Butcher was a reasonably healthy woman.

Constable Williams described the scene of the crime and in reply to a juror's question, stated that 'The deceased was a woman of light character. I have seen her with a man in an outhouse, and she was a likely person to meet a man by appointment. She would not be likely to have men in her house, as her landlord would turn her out if he heard of any such conduct.' The inquest was adjourned to Thursday 26 March.

There was much discussion about the motive for the crime and robbery was ruled out because Ruth Butcher was known to have been quite poverty stricken. A local newspaper reported that a day or two before her death Ruth had been heard to say that she would like a piece of bacon but could not afford it. There was also speculation 'that the only reasonable solution seemed to be that the deceased met with some man, that they went down the lane together, that he gave her the piece of bacon as a consideration for an immoral return (for it is said that she had no money at all that day), that the man and the woman quarrelled, that the former struck the latter and having injured the woman more seriously that he intended, the murderer suddenly resolved to silence the only living witness to his brutality and beat out her brains with a stone.'

Ruth Butcher was laid to rest in an unmarked pauper's grave in the east side of North Perrott churchyard at noon on Friday 20 March in a coffin supplied by the parish on which was inscribed 'R.B., aged 42, 1874'. The service was performed by Mr Down and Ruth's two children were present with some 50 local women and children; Annie was crying bitterly but Ruth's son, John, took little notice of the proceedings. It was said that the boy's feet protruded through his boots and his clothing indicated the wretched poverty in which he lived. Local people for many years maintained that the earth never settled after the grave was filled in.

On the following Sunday, because of the sensation of the murder, it was recorded that 'the scene was visited by a large number of persons, the village being thronged from morn to night. Some of the inhabitants estimated that the number of strangers was between three and four thousand. Many of the visitors carried away sprigs of thorn stained with blood, and so great was the demand for these relics of the tragedy that some of the bushes were almost demolished.'

The adjourned inquest was held on the 26 March and since the only evidence presented was that of Superintendent Everitt relating to the reward, the matter was adjourned again until the 20 April when the Coroner was informed that despite the most intense searching, no further clues to the murder had been found. Superintendent Everitt explained that several leads had been followed up and eliminated. The home of a possible suspect in Crewkerne had been thoroughly searched but nothing suspicious was found. Another lead had pointed to a man who had lived with Ruth Butcher, and daughter Annie had been called to give evidence of the rows between the man and her mother. However, the unnamed man had left the deceased's house over six weeks before and the police reported that a warrant had been out some time prior to the murder for his arrest for deserting his own children.

The police asked for no further adjournment as the Chief Constable considered it would be undesirable to keep the inquest open for any longer. The jury then returned a verdict of 'Wilful Murder against some person or persons unknown' and gave their fees for the purchase of clothing for Ruth's daughter; her brother having already been taken into the care of the parish. In the report of the proceedings of the final adjournment of the inquest, the local press mentioned that it had been reported in the village that a carpenter from neighbouring Misterton, 'whose mind had been much affected by the murder', had died during the previous night from inflammation of the lungs for which he had been attended by Dr Cox.

The murderer of the hapless Ruth Butcher was never found but somewhere, and perhaps not too far away, a man took to his grave the ghastly secret of a terrible night in March 1874. Was it all for a piece of bacon?

'NOTHING HAS EVER BEEN ADMINISTERED TO HER IN HER FOOD'

The public-houses and drawing rooms of Yeovil were full of gossip and rumour in the second weekend of July 1860. Sarah Peters, the sickly young wife of a respectable linen draper, had died in agony in somewhat mysterious circumstances and an inquest was being held. It was being said that because Dr Garland, the Peters' physician, had been concerned at his patient's condition, he had sent a sample of her water to Bristol to be analysed by Mr William Herapath, an eminent Professor of Chemistry and toxicologist, and the results had shown traces of a poison.

Sarah Peters died at about one o'clock in the morning of Thursday 5 July 1860 after suffering violent sickness and diarrhoea accompanied by severe stomach pain over a period of several weeks which had been diagnosed by Dr Garland as an 'intense irritation of the stomach and bowels of an obscure nature'. He found that his patient would improve for a few days but then relapse and so, with the consent of her husband, Silvester, the doctor had taken the sample of urine in which Mr Herapath had discovered the poison antimony. Alarmed at the report when he received it on 2 July, Dr Garland immediately informed Mr Smith, the Superintendent of Yeovil Police.

The doctor visited his patient the following day and was surprised, when on enquiring whether Sarah was taking her medicine, to be told by her husband that she was not because he had considered it better for her to stop. Mr Peters hoped that the doctor would not be offended. Doctor Garland strongly disagreed as he could see no improvement and in view of the Herapath report asked to be allowed to visit again the next day. Mr Peters initially refused the request, stating that doctors were very expensive, but changed his mind when Dr Garland offered to visit as a friend.

The doctor was called to the Peters' home over their High Street shop during the evening of 4 July and found the patient in extreme agony. During the night he continued to visit and apply all the remedies he could but the pain did not cease and Sarah died the next morning. An inquest was ordered and the coroner, D.H. Ashford Esq, 'assisted by a highly respectable jury', opened the proceedings in the Mermaid Inn on Saturday 7 July.

After the jury had viewed the body, the first witness to be called was Dr Garland, who told of the last days of Sarah Peters and of his suspicions. He also presented the letter from Mr Herapath giving the results of the tests on the urine sample. The coroner then adjourned the inquest and ordered a post mortem on the deceased despite objection from Mr Glyde, a Yeovil solicitor retained by Mr Peters, who believed this to be unnecesary. Mr Jay, a surgeon from Queen Camel, was appointed to carry out this task 'in order that no misunderstandings might occur amongst the medical profession in the town'! However, Mr Jay was found to be away from home, and the post mortem was carried out by Mr Winter Walter, a surgeon from Stoke-sub-Hamdon, assisted by Dr Garland and his partner, Dr Thorpe. Also present was Dr Russell Aldridge, West Coker surgeon Mr John Moore, and Dr Taylor Warry, the last named retained to represent Mr Peters' interest.

The adjourned inquest resumed in the Mermaid Inn on Tuesday 24 July when evidence was taken from Mr Walter on his post mortem. He stated that the lungs of the deceased were in the primary stages of consumption with many tubercles present, there was extensive mesenteric disease in the abdomen, and the liver, which was in a very poor state, the duodenum and the colon were glued together by massive inflammation which formed the seat of an abscess. This had breached the colon allowing some of its contents to escape into the peritoneum and the resulting peritonitis was the immediate cause of death. Mr Walter stated that he could find no trace of poison in the body but at the request of Dr Garland the stomach and internal organs were sealed in jars and handed to Superintendent Smith who took them to Mr Herapath in Bristol.

Dr Garland was recalled and confirmed the findings of Mr Walter. He elaborated on the condition of Sarah Peters' body which was very emaciated but he considered that the perforation of the colon might have been caused by a harmful substance.

The evidence of the next witness was awaited with much expectation. Mr William Herapath was one of the foremost chemists and toxicologists of the day and the sixty-four-year-old professor had gained a formidable reputation over the past quarter of a century since he appeared for the prosecution at the trial of husband poisoner Mrs Clara Smith in 1835. He confirmed that the sample of urine taken from Sarah Peters contained antimony but there was no sign of the poison or any other metallic or mineral irritant in the organs sent to him. The stomach was inflamed in two places in a patchy manner, as were two places in the intestines, and this was usually found in cases of irritant poisoning. He explained that in instances of a general inflammatory disease the whole organ would be inflamed. The chemist went on to say that inflammation produced by an irritant was influenced by the nature of the substance, if solid it would operate in a very local place but, if fluid, it would only act in the lower portions of the organ. There was, in his opinion, sufficient inflammation in the stomach and intestines to cause death.

When asked why, if antimony was found in the dead woman's urine, there was no sign of the poison in her tissues, Mr Herapath stated that in the few days which had passed between the sample and death there was sufficient time for the poison to leave the system. All he could assume was that the antimony had passed away even though, the appearance of the intestines indicated an irritant had been at work.

Mr Herapath now dropped a minor bombshell. He stated, in reply to a question from a juror, that he had never seen a liver in such a poor condition as that of Mrs Peters (and he 'had seen hundreds') and this must have been the result of a long standing disease; also he had never known antimony to be a cause of death. The chemist then qualified this last remark by pointing out that it had not yet been discovered how long antimony remained in the body or how long it took to disappear because it had been identified as a poison only recently. Mr Herapath also pointed out that antimony was sometimes given medically to induce vomiting but the inflammation seen in Mrs Peters' organs would never be produced by such small doses.

Dr Garland was recalled once again and confirmed that he had not prescribed any medicine which contained antimony. Sarah had told him that the sickness came on almost immediately after she had taken gruel, or the arrowroot he had prescribed, and complained that the medicine was making her ill. He stated that he had assured her that this was impossible because the preparations he was giving her was one of the strongest against sickness. Dr Garland asked Sarah how soon she was sick after taking her medicine and she replied that it was within half an hour but then she added that she took some gruel during this time. The doctor gave her some more medicine, waited with her for half an hour and then told her not to take anything for another hour. When he called the next morning he found that Mrs Peters had suffered no sickness.

Dr Garland recounted that when his patient died he had suggested to Mr Peters that as the cause was obscure an examination should be held. The widower would not agree and exclaimed that he would rather have his own bowels opened than his wife's should be touched. The doctor assured Mr Peters that he had no suspicion that anything was wrong but despite this he would not give consent. However during the discussion Mr Peters suddenly remarked, 'You know Mr Garland, nothing has ever been administered to her in her food.' Taken aback, the doctor left the room, only to return after consulting his partner to say that he had received the report from Mr Herapath indicating poison in the urine sample and because he did not know how it got there he would not issue a death certificate. Mr Peters once again refused to permit an examination and said that he would get a certificate from Dr Tomkyns. Dr Garland then went to the police.

During the proceedings, Mr Langworthy, a solicitor from Ilminster who was now acting for Mr Peters, had asked questions of the witnesses from time to time seeking clarification of the evidence. He now requested that Mr Walter be recalled and asked him to tell how many perforations he had seen in the intestines. The surgeon replied that he had found two or three which he concluded had been caused by the escape of matter from the large abscess and did not arise from anything within the organ.

The inquest was adjourned once again to the following Saturday to enable the remaining medical men who had attended the post mortem to give evidence.

At precisely 10 am on Saturday the coroner and the jury re-assembled in the Mermaid Inn. Evidence was taken from Dr Aldridge who confirmed the findings of his medical colleagues and expressed the opinion that the inflammation and resulting peritonitis was caused by disease; he conceded, however, that the administration of an acute irritant could cause peritonitis. In reply to a question from Mr Langworthy, the doctor stated his belief that Mrs Peters had suffered from a fatal consumptive disease for several months and the symptoms of sickness were usual in such illness.

Doctors Warry and Thorpe and Mr Moore, the surgeon, next gave their testimonies on the post mortem and supported the opinion that death was the result of peritonitis. To support his opinion that the vomiting from which Mrs Peters suffered was the result of her general illness, Dr Warry stated that her husband had given him a letter she had written on 24 May, during a stay at Worle, near Weston-super-Mare, telling him that she was having bouts of sickness. However, Mr Moore was not completely certain of the cause and was at a loss to account for the patchy nature of the inflammation; it could be, he said, the result of an irritant such as antimony. The jury now adjourned and after deciding to seek no further evidence the coroner summed up.

He remarked that there was considerable evidence that the intestines of the deceased had been perforated and the body considerably diseased. It would be for the jury to consider whether or not they thought the disease was sufficient to account for the perforation. Mr Herapath's evidence that antimony had got into the system had been corroborated by Mr Moore and the jury would have to consider whether this had anything to do with producing the perforation or causing death. The jury then retired to consider their verdict.

They had heard how Sarah Peters had died in agony after a painful illness over several months; how her doctor could not be certain of the cause and was suspicious; how his suspicions were confirmed when traces of the poison antimony were found in the sample of urine taken before death; how an eminent toxicologist could find no trace of any poison in the body even though he was certain that a substance had been at work; and how the cause of death was peritonitis caused by the escape of some contents through holes in the intestine. But, although the reason for the breaches in the intestine could be explained as being the work of a gross irritant, they could also be the natural result of the consumptive disease from which Sarah Peters suffered. The jury were therefore faced with disease as being the most likely cause of death but with the suspicion that something more sinister had been at work to hasten poor Sarah to the grave. They came to what, perhaps, was the only verdict in the circumstances and did not take long to return it.

'Sarah Peters died from a complication of disease accelerated by the presence of some irritant, but how or by whom administered there is no evidence before the jury to show'.

No doubt Mr Silvester Peters breathed a sigh of relief at the verdict but it was left open for the gossip and rumour-mongers to make the most of the words, 'how or by whom administered'. Silvester Peters' linen draper's shop was in the part of Yeovil now known as The Boro' and he is included in *Kelly's Directory* for the town in 1861 but is no longer present in the *Kelly's Post Office Directory* of 1866. In the 1861 census return the Peters' household included, Silvester, widower, thirty-two, born at Worle; his three-year-old daughter, Augusta Matilda; Matilda Bailey, unmarried, twenty-six described as a 'Lady', born at Blagdon, together with shop assistant Gilbert Poole and Mary Ann Skeats the servant.

Incidentally, antimony is used in the dyeing of cloth.

THE DEVIL OF
DEADMAN'S POST

John Ball was hurrying over Staple Hill to Buckland St Mary in the early evening of Friday 23 April, 1830 when he espied Farmer James Lane standing by the hedge of his potato field. As he came closer Farmer Lane called out – 'John come over, I've a dead fellow here!' – 'Who is it?' enquired the puzzled John Ball as he scrambled over the hedge. 'T'is our Jack,' replied the farmer pointing to the small figure of a boy huddled faced down on the wet earth.

John Ball knelt down by the still form and turning it over saw that it was the farmer's twelve-year-old son John and was relieved to see that the child was breathing.

'Come on lad, try and stand up,' he whispered kindly.

'I can't,' was the faint reply.

'Jack, try and get up and go home,' coaxed John Ball.

'I've tried and I can't,' whimpered the child.

With this John Ball raised the lad and sat him back against the hedge bank. However before he could lend any further assistance, Farmer Lane took over and shouted at his son, 'If you don't get up and go over thik hedge I'll take a good stick to ee!' When the boy didn't move Lane grabbed him by the collar, hauled him to the top of the hedge and dropped his son 6 feet into the waterfilled ditch below. The horrified John Ball scrambled after the child and gently pulled him out of the ditch and laid him down on the roadside bank. Turning to Farmer Lane, who had now jumped down from the hedge, Ball shouted, 'This boy is as good as dead!' 'There's nothing the matter with 'in', was the terse reply and, pulling his son to his feet, Lane punched the boy hard on his forehead.

By now three other local men, James Cross, James Quick and George Bryant, had arrived on the scene and witnessed the beating. Farmer Lane brought his horse from the field and threw the semi-conscious boy across its back but after travelling a few yards John lost his tenuous grip. Lane dragged his son from the horse and throwing him over his shoulder like a bag of the potatoes he had been planting carried the child the rest of the way to their home at Deadman's Post. At seven o'clock the next morning, 24 April, John Lane's short and miserable life quietly came to an end and two days later an inquest was held into his death before the coroner, Mr Caines and 'a respectable jury' in the Castle Inn on Neroche Hill. After hearing the evidence of the witnesses to the assaults on the boy and the medical testimony of two Chard surgeons, Mr Wheadon and Mr Spicer, the jury returned a verdict of wilful murder against Farmer James Lane and he was arrested and committed to Ilchester Gaol to await trial.

Pleading not guilty, James Lane went on trial for his life four months later on Friday 20 August, 1830 at the Somerset Summer Assizes, charged with the 'wilful murder of John Lane by inflicting blows, throwing him with violence to the ground and not providing him with sufficient food.' The trial would reveal a story of beatings, starvation and the awful ill-usage of the farmer's son over many years and in the end death may well have come as a friend to the child.

John Ball was the first witness called for the prosecution and he described the brutal events of 23 April on Staple Hill and went on to tell how John had been treated when he finally reached his home at Deadman's Post. On entering Farmer Lane had dropped the boy off his back onto the floor shouting, 'Lie there you damned sulky young beggar, I'll never pick 'ee up no more!' Hearing the commotion, Mrs Lane, appeared and, picking up her son, carried him across the room and laid him down in front of the fire. The witness then recounted how Farmer Lane had grabbed John and placed his head within a few inches of the flames shouting 'I'll see whether he'll move now or not!' The boy cried out in fear and pain but he was too weak to move his head away from the scorching heat. John Ball ran across the room and pulled the child away from the fire back to where his mother had laid him. Farmer Lane, however, had not finished with his son for he grabbed him by his coat collar and dragged him to the oppo-site end of the room away from any warmth, muttering, 'You shan't lay there comforting yerself.'

John Ball explained to the Court that he had been growing more concerned for the boy and told Farmer Lane in no uncertain terms not to treat his son in this way and that he should put him to bed for he feared that John might die. The farmer had answered callously that 'this would be a good riddance and he wished to God that the boy would be dead before morning.' The witness went on to tell how he tried to give John some food but because the boy's teeth were so tightly clenched, this proved unsuccessful. Later, when John Ball left the farm, he told Lane that he feared that the next time he would hear of Jack he would be dead. On cross-examination the witness confirmed that young John Lane was 'a weak, sulky and lazy boy and had run away from home on several occasions.' However Ball believed that if the lad had been in good health 'dropping him into the ditch would not have hurt him.'

Next to give evidence was James Cross who was the first of the other three witnesses to the brutality on Staple Hill. He told how he had seen Farmer Lane and his son planting potatoes and went on to describe how the father had dragged the boy to the top of the hedge and dropped him into the ditch, how he had shaken and then punched the child on the forehead with his clenched fist. James Quick, the next witness, confirmed what James Cross had described but added that he had heard that Farmer Lane's son was very sulky and used to run away.

The last of the trio, George Bryant, now gave evidence and stated that when he arrived on the scene at Staple Hill, John Lane was lying in the road. He had asked what had happened and was told by Farmer Lane that the boy had fallen down in a fit 'as usual.' Bryant stated that he had then told the father, ' I fear this is a bad job and I hear that you use your son very ill. The boy will die and then there will be a coroner's inquest and you'll suffer for it: he will die.' 'I wish he may be dead before morning', was Farmer Lane's retort. George Bryant went on to say that when he had seen young John Lane some seven or eight weeks earlier he appeared to be in a poor state for want of food. In reply to a question under cross-examination, the witness confirmed that he had seen other boys look pale and thin but, he emphasised, they had not been starved. Bryant added that he had given John food on that occasion because he had run away from his father.

Robert Foxwell, who was lodging at the Lane's farm, next gave evidence. He recounted how he had arrived home at Deadman's Post at about eight o'clock on the fatal evening and had seen John lying on the floor in a corner of the room looking very ill. He had asked him what was the matter but had received no reply. Foxwell stated that John had been in a weak state for some time and he had seen his father beat him with large sticks. He also told how the boy's mother, only three weeks before, had begged her husband not to thrash the youngster or he would kill her son. Under cross-examination the witness agreed that he had frequently seen farmer's boys beaten as much.

Last to give evidence was William Ball who had also been lodging at Deadman's Post at the time of John Lane's death. He confirmed the beatings the boy had received from his father and that several times during the Monday and Tuesday of the week preceeding his demise, the boy had been beaten with a large stick, knocked to the ground and kicked. Ball had begged the farmer to stop beating his son but the reply had always been that 'he was a bad boy.' He also recalled that one Sunday some twelve months before his death, John had been hung up by his wrists as a punishment for running away, and there were many days when the boy was given little or no food. Cross-examined, William Ball confirmed that he had owed money for his lodgings, but denied that Farmer Lane had told him to leave if he did not pay. He stated that he had seen idle boys beaten but never so much or with such large sticks as when the prisoner beat his son. The last witness had now given evidence and the lawyers for both sides went into conference following which Farmer Lane was asked if he wished to withdraw his plea of not guilty to the indictment for murder. This he did on the advice of his Counsel and pleaded guilty to manslaughter; the murder charge was then dropped. Thus James Lane escaped the gallows but was transported to Australia for life.

THE UNTIMELY END OF CONSTABLE PENNY

Constable William Hubbard of the Yeovil Police was late for duty. It was now a quarter-past midnight on the morning of Sunday 12 January, 1862, and the constable knew that his colleague waiting outside the Quicksilver Mail on the top of Hendford Hill would have a few words to say about punctuality when he finally arrived.

Constable Hubbard had heard the shouting and laughing before he began to climb the road leading up the hill and soon the bright moonlight picked out a group of not too sober men. Navvy George Hansford had enjoyed his Saturday evening drinking in the Railway Inn at the bottom of Hendford Hill, and, in company with George Chant, Charles Rogers and about a dozen other navvies, he was making a noisy way home.

William Hubbard wished the revellers a curt goodnight as he passed but received in return catcalls and some swearing. The constable ignored the insults and did not react to the jostling from George Hansford as he passed by. He had walked but a few yards when there was a clatter of falling objects in front of him, followed by cheering from behind. Hubbard swung around just in time to see George Hansford pick up a stone and throw it at him. The constable had no time to duck but Hansford's aim was poor and although he was standing only a few yards away from the officer the stone missed. Several more stones were thrown, and deciding that discretion was the better part of valour William Hubbard turned about and with the jeers of the navvies ringing in his ears he made his way quickly up the hill to where Constable Penny was waiting

William Penny was well known and respected in Yeovil but during recent years he had suffered much personal tragedy. His wife had been committed to a lunatic asylum and his two young children upon whom he doted were living with relatives in Wincanton. Constable Penny was not, however, a man to avoid his duty, and following the report from the breathless Hubbard he was determined to take the offending stone thrower into custody.

The group of navvies eventually came up to the two officers and as they passed, Hubbard pointed out George Hansford as the offender. Constable Penny stepped forward and placing his hand on Hansford's shoulder demanded his name. 'Sandle,' was the reply, and with this Constable Hubbard charged him with throwing stones and ordered him to accompany the two officers to the Yeovil Police Station. Hansford vehemently denied the accusation and, supported by his companions, refused to be taken into custody. The navvies began shouting and swearing at the officers and William Penny, realising that the situation could get out of hand, moved away and called to Hubbard to join him whispering that it was no use trying to take Hansford into custody because the men were in such an ugly mood. He suggested that the best course of action would be to go back to the Police Station and seek further assistance. As the two officers hurried away Hubbard shouted that they were going to Yeovil to get more men to take Hansford.

Sergeant Benjamin Keats was on duty in the town and, hearing the noise coming from the direction of Hendford Hill, had set out to find the cause. As he began to climb the hill he met the two constables and Penny asked for help to take Hansford into custody. The three officers set off up the hill in pursuit of the offender and his companions who could be heard making their noisy way along the Dorchester Road. By the time Sergeant Keats and the two constables had caught up with the revellers, they had reached the Red House Inn at the Barwick and East Coker cross roads. Constable Hubbard pointed out Hansford and Sergeant Keats ordered him to be taken into custody. Hansford once again refused to be arrested and Constable Penny, drawing out his handcuffs, managed to snap one of the cuffs on the navvy's right wrist. Hansford shouted for help but only George Chant and Charles Rogers came to his aid; the rest made off into the night wanting nothing more to do with the events they could see coming.

Chant and Roger, being strong hard men, piled into the three policemen in an endeavour to free their companion. Rogers produced a thick stick and struck William Penny a savage blow on his head, smashing his hat flat and spinning the officer across the road. He then struck Keats on the back of his head, splitting his hat and knocking him to the ground. Constable Hubbard, springing to the aid of his Sergeant, was in turn struck in the face by the heavy weapon wielded by Rogers who, realising what he had done, turned and fled. Hubbard, a big man, quickly recovered from the blow and with blood pouring down his face went after his assailant. A running fight took place which resulted in Rogers being felled by a massive blow from the enraged constable. The fight was knocked out of

Rogers, who pleaded not to be struck again as Hubbard picked him up by his collar and marched him towards the Red House Inn.

Sergeant Keats had been temporarily stunned but as his senses returned he saw, to his horror, William Penny lying on the ground being savagely beaten by Hansford and Chant. He shouted to Penny to get up and as he moved to help the fallen officer, the two navvies broke off their battering and ran. Keats, by now fully recovered, charged after them and dragged down Hansford who gave no further resistance. Chant continued to run and made his escape into the night. Returning with his prisoner the Sergeant was horrified at the condition of the injured Penny and shouted to Hubbard for help.

On hearing the call Hubbard released Rogers, who quickly slipped away, and ran to help his Sergeant. The two men gently lifted their companion and carried the badly beaten Penny into the inn where Mrs Rendall, the landlady, made him comfortable in her parlour. Blood was pouring from wounds on the injured policeman's head and Hubbard was despatched to Yeovil for medical assistance.

When Dr Garland arrived he found William Penny in a state of collapse but, following the administration of brandy and water, the patient rallied and sat up. The doctor's examination revealed three deep lacerations to the skull, his left ear was nearly severed and there was bruising to the constable's head. Dr Garland could not detect any fractures and although Penny frequently vomited, he became lucid and asked to go home to West Coker. The doctor refused the request and the injured man was put to bed at the inn.

William Penny was visited again by Dr Garland the following morning and although he asked to go home the doctor advised him to stay at the Red House for a few more days until he was fully recovered. The constable was, however, a stubborn man and, contrary to Garland's advice, he went home by cart that Monday afternoon. In the meantime, George Hansford had been lodged in the town gaol and George Chant arrested in bed in his lodgings at Stoford; Charles Rogers was still on the run.

Six days after the Dorchester Road fight, the assault on the police became a capital offence for Constable William Penny died on Saturday afternoon, 18 January.

On Tuesday 21 January 1862 the inquest on the late Constable Penny was held in the New Inn at West Coker before the coroner, Dr Wybrants. Following an account of the fight from the two surviving officers and medical evidence from Dr Garland, the jury returned a verdict of wilful murder against George Hansford, George Chant, and, in his absence, Charles Rogers who had been identified as the third assailant. On Friday 24 January, Hansford and Chant were brought before the town magistrates and charged with the assault and wilful murder of Police Constable William Penny; both prisoners pleaded not guilty and were remanded in custody for trial at the forthcoming spring Assizes.

Charles Rogers did not remain at liberty for long and was captured on the morning of Saturday 25 January. He was hiding in the stables of the Greyhound Inn at Dorchester. On his arrest by Superintendent Pouncey of the Dorset Constabulary, Rogers stated plaintively that he had hit Constable Hubbard because 'if I had not hit he, he would a' killed I.' Rogers was brought before the Yeovil magistrates later that day and similarly charged with assaulting the police and the wilful murder of William Penny. The prisoner pleaded not guilty and was remanded in custody to stand trial with his two companions.

The trial began on Monday 31 March 1862 before the Honourable Sir Colin Blackburn, a Justice of the Queen's Bench, with Mr Cole and Mr Hooper leading for the Crown and Mr Ffooks defending. Mr Cole opened the case for the prosecution and Sergeant Keats and Constable Hubbard recounted the events of 12 January.

Dr Garland gave the medical evidence and under cross-examination stated that the cause of death was a fractured skull. In the doctor's opinion, although the fracture resulted from a blow by a blunt instrument, he believed that a handcuff was more likely to have caused the major injury rather than a stick. He also admitted that he did not discover the fracture until the post-mortem because fractures were difficult to diagnose. However the doctor rebuffed suggestions that Penny had contributed to his demise by leaving the Red House Inn against his medical advice and expressed the strong opinion that death had been inevitable.

Mr Ffooks opened the defence by submitting that the stone throwing had not been of a serious or malicious nature, and Constable Hubbard had issued no warnings nor taken any action against those involved. The original offence was of a minor nature and he did not believe that the constable had any apprehension or sense of danger at the time. Mr Ffooks pointed out that three-quarters of an hour had elapsed between the stones being thrown and the attempted arrest outside the inn. He submitted that during that time the police officers had not been in the continual pursuit of the alleged culprit, nor had there been a continual apprehension of danger. Unless these circumstances were present, the police officers had no right to arrest George Hansford and therefore the three men were justified in resisting what to all intents was an illegal arrest and in using such force as might be necessary to prevent this.

In response the prosecution contended that the pursuit had never been abandoned because, when the stone throwing took place, Constable Hubbard, judging himself to be seriously outnumbered by his assailants, went to obtain assistance and renewed the pursuit immediately he met with Constable Penny. At this stage of the proceedings the trial was adjourned until nine o'clock the next morning.

The next day Mr Ffooks proceeded to address the jury and stated that one of the main points they would have to ask themselves before reaching a verdict was whether there was any assault committed by the prisoners in the first place when the stones were thrown. If there was no assault, then the police were acting in exaggeration of their duty in attempting to arrest Hansford for a minor misdemeanour and for which they had no such right. Therefore, if they had no lawful right of arrest, he believed the men were not guilty of murder but of a justifiable homicide! Mr Ffooks contended that if there was no intention to commit an assault when the stones were thrown at the constable then no assault was committed. There was he said, no intention on the part of the prisoners to assault the policeman and they were proceeding quietly to their homes.

Mr Ffooks then went on to point out to the jury that it was generally supposed that to make a person responsible for a criminal act there must be an intention. He submitted that in this case there was no such intention to assault the police or any intention to cause reasonable apprehension of danger. With regard to the question of continual pursuit, Mr Ffooks suggested that it was reasonable to infer that Constable Hubbard had hastened to the top of the hill after the stones were thrown not to get help, but because it was his duty to be there at midnight and he was late. He considered that the police had been led astray by their anxiety to get a conviction and had been guilty of a great exaggeration. Mr Ffooks maintained that this was an unlawful aggression by the policemen upon the liberty of the three men and who, he claimed, possessing the proud name of Englishmen, would not be provoked to resist? These men would deserve the scorn of everyone if they had not resisted and it would be impossible for the most benign of philosophers not to do so under such circumstances! The men had acted with great forbearance, and had refrained from exercising any unnecessary violence in defending their liberty.

Defending counsel referred particularly to George Chant who had endeavoured to take the stick from Rogers so that he might not use it improperly. All the circumstances proved that there was no preconceived design and therefore Mr Ffooks submitted that in this case the law of common intent did not apply. If the jury found Chant guilty of this serious offence on the testimony which had been produced it would be a verdict which would not meet with the approval of anyone who had heard the trial. He believed, with confidence, that when the jury had considered all the evidence, they would not feel justified in bringing a guilty verdict against Chant. With regard to Hansford and Rogers, Mr Ffooks stated that they had no weapon which could be termed deadly. They had merely used those weapons which nature had given them to resist unlawful arrest and his clients could never have expected, or contemplated, that the unhappy Penny would have been hurled into eternity.

Mr Ffooks pointed out that the law threw around the police in their arduous duties a peculiar protection and powers and they should operate them with proper moderation. In conclusion, Mr Ffooks contended that what had happened had been brought about by the foolish conduct of the police in the first instance and he felt confident therefore that the jury would not find the prisoners guilty of the crime of wilful murder.

In his summing up, the Judge explained to the jury that there were many distinctions with respect to an arrest. A policeman had a right to arrest on suspicion of a felony, but in the less serious case of a misdemeanour, he had no such power to arrest purely on the suspicion of a misdemeanour having been committed. In the latter case the policeman's duty was to go to the magistrates and obtain a warrant. A policeman could only arrest for a misdemeanour if the offence was committed in his sight and upon the spot and in fresh pursuit. It was to be much regretted that Constable Hubbard did not wait until the next day and then go to Yeovil magistrates to obtain a warrant, in which case the unfortunate death of William Penny would never have occured. Unless the jury found these questions in favour of the prosecution, the capital part of the charge failed. Then, if not guilty of murder, were the defendants guilty of manslaughter? It appeared to the Judge that there was nothing in the evidence which would reduce the charge below that. If the offence was manslaughter, were the defendants all guilty, or only one or more of them? The Judge then sent the jury to consider their verdict.

After a considerable absence, the jury found George Hansford guilty of manslaughter with a recommendation of mercy on account of the police having exceeded their duty. Chant and Rogers were acquitted, but were then indicted for assaulting Sergeant Keats and Constable Hubbard in the execution of their duty. The Judge stated, however, that in view of the verdict on Hansford he would order an acquittal as the jury had decided that the police were not executing their duty. Both defendants were then acquitted. Later in the day the Judge sentenced George Hansford to four years penal servitude.

Constable William Penny was buried in West Coker churchyard on Wednesday 22 January 1862. Six of his colleagues bore their comrade's coffin to its final resting place just inside the east gate where the constable's headstone can be seen to this day and which reads:

In Memory of
William Penny
Somerset County police
He died the 18th January 1862
in the 42nd year of his age
a few days after receiving severe injuries
in the execution of his duty.
This stone has been erected by some
inhabitants of this Parish as a mark
of their deep regret at his untimely
end and also as a tesimony of their great
respect for a faithful public servant.

THE KILLING OF DANDY JOE

It was the beginning of the third week of August, 1843 and Yeovil was in a state of much excitement. There were rumours that Joseph 'Dandy Joe' Seymour, well known for the ready use of his fists, was dead, killed it was said by 'unfair means at the hands of a respectable farmer named John Hodges'.

On 17 August the town heard the story as it unfolded before the coroner, R.P. Caines Esq., and his 'respectable' jury at the inquest in the Castle Inn. First to give evidence was Farmer James Bewsey of Adber who recounted that on the previous Saturday afternoon he had been drinking at the White Post Inn on Rimpton Hill between Sherborne and Marston Magna and at about 3 pm he had gone into the skittle alley where John Hodges and Dandy Joe Seymour were skittling for sixpence and a pint. A row had just broken out between Farmer Hodges and Dandy Joe over the winnings of a game and Joe's fifteen-year-old son, Charles, had joined in. This was too much for the farmer who told young Seymour that if he was his son he would 'give him a cut or two with a stick!'. Without warning, according to James Bewsey, Dandy Joe punched Hodges in the face and sent him spinning across the alley. As the farmer fell he struck his head on the wall and the crown of his hat was broken in two by the force of the blow. For several minutes Hodges lay dazed on the floor until, recovering, he was helped to his feet by Farmer Bewsey and told that Dandy Joe had put him down. By now Dandy Joe, fuelled by cider and beer, was in fighting mood and challenged the farmer to fight. Hodges refused for at that moment he was in no condition to accept the invitation and Joe rushed out of the alley swearing and cursing.

The story was then taken up by John Willis, of the Marston Inn, and a local thatcher, Jonathan Biddiscombe. The two men were returning home from Sherborne and, feeling thirsty, had stopped their cart outside the White Post when Dandy Joe erupted from the Inn. They recounted how he had stormed into the road and stood shouting abuse at John Hodges who now emerged from the skittle alley.

'Damn thy eyes, come out here and I'll give thee a belly full or thee shall I', he yelled.

The fully recovered Farmer Hodges went out into the road, and standing in front of Dandy Joe, who was adopting various boxing attitudes, demanded, 'Why did you hit me? I never gave thee any anger, thou hast nearly hit my brains out' and, turning to Jonathan Biddiscombe, the farmer pointed to his broken hat exclaiming, 'Look 'ere John, he has hit my hat all to pieces and stunned me!'

Turning once again to Dandy Joe, the farmer called, 'I was never hit by a man in my life without returning it and I won't be hit by thee!' He then advanced towards his opponent and landed a single blow on Seymour's right eye. The main road outside the White Post was on a steep slope and Dandy Joe was knocked backwards down the hill, striking his head as he hit the ground.

Jonathan Biddiscombe stated that he had helped Dandy Joe to his feet and pointed out that in his opinion the farmer's punch had been a light one and if Joe had been standing on level ground he would not have fallen. Both Biddiscombe and Willis told the jury that they knew Farmer Hodges to be a steady and quiet man whereas Dandy Joe Seymour was a 'fighting man' and 'bore a bad character for his fighting propensity'.

The next witness was Dandy Joe's son, Charles, who gave a detailed account of the dispute in the skittle alley. This was very different from that of Farmer Bewsey and if accepted, could place John Hodges in peril.

The lad recounted that on the Saturday morning he had accompanied his father to the Hodges' farm at Adber where they had enjoyed a meal of bread and cheese, washed down with cider and then adjourned to the White Post Inn. From mid-morning until about three o'clock in the afternoon the three remained drinking beer and finally began to play skittles for sixpence and a pint per game.

Charles described how his father had knocked down several pins but then Farmer Hodges refused to continue with the game, and assuming the bet won, Dandy Joe had picked up the two sixpenny pieces stake money and put them in his pocket. At this, according to young Seymour, the farmer grabbed Joe by his neckerchief, shaking him, and demanding his money back. Charles shouted at Hodges to let his father go but the enraged farmer threatened to beat the boy for his cheek. Dandy Joe managed to free himself and struck out at John Hodges, knocking him over. As Joe left the alley, the farmer was on his feet and another scuffle took place which resulted in Hodges being struck to the floor where he remained for several minutes. Charles went on to describe how the two men met again in the bar where they both hit each other and his father was knocked off the stool on which he had just sat. After this episode the two went out and fought again in the road.

As if to impress his honesty on the jury, young Seymour told them that he had 'been to church once and chapel two or three times in the past five years'. This was a very different story of the dispute but the evidence of George Long, the landlord of the White Post, would support that given by Farmer Bewsey.

Long described how he had heard the disturbance and, as he entered the skittle alley, saw Dandy Joe punch John Hodges to the ground; at no time did he see the farmer grab Seymour's neckerchief or provoke him in any way. The landlord went on to say that the two men left the alley but he did not follow them as he went to collect empty glasses from the back yard and saw nothing of the scuffle in the road. With his nose bleeding, Dandy Joe had been helped back into the inn, and, after he had been cleaned up, he went out into the garden where he remained lying down for several hours. The witness had kept an eye on Seymour during the afternoon but was not concerned at his state because he thought the man was 'under the influence of liquor'.

At about six o'clock, a local farmer, George Lockyer, brought Dandy Joe back into the inn and with the help of the Rimpton constable, James Bishop, they sat him down in the parlour where he remained in a semi-conscious condition for the rest of the evening. By ten o'clock Seymour was no different, but still believing he was half drunk, Landlord Long and the constable put him to bed. Young Charles had stayed with his father and spent the night with him locked up in the dark in a small room. This was a usual precaution, the landlord explained, so that a drunk could not wander about the inn or set fire to it by knocking over the candle provided for sober guests.

The next witness was John Bishop, the Rimpton constable, who stated that he had been called to the inn early on Sunday morning because the landlord was concerned at Seymour's condition; there was blood on the bed clothes and the man seemed no better. Bishop sent young Charles back to Yeovil for his mother and just before mid-day she arrived with both her sons to collect her husband. However, when Mrs Long, the landlord's wife, suggested that a doctor should be called for Joe, Mrs Seymour declined and said that she had seen him beaten a great deal worse'.

Dandy Joe Seymour remained at the White Post during the Sunday afternoon talking occasionally to his wife and eating some biscuits and gruel. At about 7 pm a horse and cart arrived and the Seymours departed for Yeovil with Joe lying on a bed of straw.

On Monday, Surgeon Markes Lambe was called to the Seymour's

home where he found Dandy Joe unconscious and, having been told of the fight, he concluded that the patient was suffering from 'concussion of the brain with extravasation of blood'. He visited Seymour on four occasions and bled him three times during the day but his efforts were in vain and Dandy Joe died at eleven o'clock on Monday night.

Surgeon Lambe told the inquest that in his opinion the cause of death was concussion of the brain and this could arise from a fall or a blow to the eye or any part of the head. No evidence was taken from Farmer John Hodges, who had been taken into custody following the death of Joseph Seymour, and was awaiting the verdict of the jury; murder would mean death, manslaughter would mean a long term of penal servitude.

The jury did not take long to return the verdict of justifiable homicide' and John Hodges was released. Dandy Joe Seymour was buried the next day.

WHO KILLED MR STUCKEY?

Early in August, 1830, Benjamin Hebditch of Over Stratton near South Petherton, wrote in his journal that his boyhood friend, 'Mr Simeon Stuckey of Chard, Builder etc, left our house about 10 o'clock at night for Chard but when he got about 20 yards beyond the second stream of water or bridge beyond Grinevids Knap and about 50 yards this side of the little cottage on the left hand side of the road he was met about eleven o'clock by some robbers who not only robbed him but murdered him and also took away his body and for several days there was many scores if not hundreds in search for the body but all in vain.'

At about four o'clock in the afternoon of Monday 9 August 1830, Mr Simeon Stuckey, a reputable builder, set out from his home in Chard for the village of Over Stratton where he was superintending the building of a house. An hour later he broke his journey at the lonely Windwhistle Inn and shared a pint of cider with the landlord Lawrence Biss. Mr Stuckey did not tarry long at the inn but left after a quarter of an hour telling mine host that he would call later in the evening on his way home.

At Over Stratton the builder dealt with his business and visited his old friend Benjamin Hebditch whom he left at about ten o'clock. Before leaving the village to return to Chard he called on his aged father who was ill in bed. Because the hour was late Simeon Stuckey only remained for a few minutes and, after promising his parents that he would see them again within the next few days, he rode off into the gathering darkness.

The shouting from the yard of the Windwhistle Inn shortly after one o'clock the next morning brought Mrs Biss to the bedroom window.

'Is the landlord there?' called the mounted figure she could just make out in the yard.

'Yes, but he's abed,' Mrs Biss replied wondering why her husband was wanted at this late hour.

'Tell him to come down at once as I want him for something particular!' was the demand from below.

By now landlord Biss was fully roused by the commotion and lighting a lamp he went down to see what all the fuss was about. Once in the yard he recognised the mounted caller as Mr Norris, the

Sheriff's officer from Crewkerne, who, pointing to a horse he was leading by the bridle, stated, 'I found this horse on Chillington Down near the clump of trees. Do you know the owner, landlord?'

Lawrence Biss inspected the animal in the light of his lamp and exclaimed, 'Know it, what don't you? Why 'tis Mr Stuckey's Old Tom!'

After carrying out a closer scrutiny of the horse, the Sheriff's officer confirmed the landlord's identification and went on to say that he had seen no one on the road between Crewkerne and Windwhistle. Somewhat puzzled at the reason for Old Tom to be wandering riderless on Chillington Common, Lawrence Biss commented that there was no sign on the bridle or the saddle that the rider had been thrown and it was therefore possible that the horse had escaped unobserved from the stable where Mr Stuckey was staying. The landlord also observed that the horse had been hot from galloping but was now quite cool.

Lawrence Biss then suggested that as Mr Norris was on his way to Chard he could take Old Tom with him and deliver the horse to Mrs Stuckey telling her what had happened. This request was rejected but as the Sheriff's officer rode off he agreed to contact Mrs Stuckey first thing in the morning. With the departure of Mr Norris the landlord removed the bridle and the saddle, turned Old Tom loose in one of his fields and went back to bed.

Lawrence Biss rose early that Tuesday morning, partook of his breakfast and, after busying himself about the inn, set off with some workmen to a local wood where they cut and hauled timber until mid-morning when the party returned home. To the landlord's surprise he found Mr Stuckey's horse still grazing contentedly in his field and telling his men of the night's events wondered aloud why Old Tom had not been called for. Biss and his party returned to the wood where they worked for the afternoon, but on returning to Windwhistle sometime after four o'clock found that the horse had still not been collected.

The landlord immediately bridled and saddled Old Tom and despatched the horse in the care of his boy to Mr Stuckey's home. Later that evening, a young man called at the inn stating that Mr Stuckey had not returned and his wife wanted to know how the horse had come into the landlord's possession. After hearing Lawrence Biss's explanation the young man rode off to Over Stratton to continue his search. By Wednesday morning, concern for the missing builder had grown and friends and acquaintances formed parties and began to search the area. Their enquiries at some cottages in Chillington which adjoined the road from Dinnington to Windwhistle, and along which Mr Stuckey would have travelled, produced a hat and a stick which were identified as belonging to the builder and which had been picked up on the road on the Tuesday morning. There were also signs of a struggle at the spot where the stick was found.

Benjamin Hebditch had joined in the search for his friend and recorded that 'we have reason to think he had about £60 with him in cash, a good watch with gold seals and a very good suit of clothes. The horse with the bridle and saddle was found near the Windwhistle Turnpike Gate, the stick, contents of his stomach and about half a pint of blood was seen by me and hundreds of others on the spot and his hat was about 100 yards this side of the brow of the hill.'

Although it was quite clear that something terrible and probably fatal had befallen Simeon Stuckey, where was the body? The intensive search along the road over which he would have travelled on his return to Chard had failed to produce any sign of the builder, either alive or dead, and in some quarters darker thoughts were being expressed. On 25 August the *Taunton Courier* ran the following story under the heading 'Alleged Murder of Stuckey at Windwhistle'

We are confirmed in our opinion upon this subject. The mysterious murder is neither a murder nor a mystery. The marks of blood, and other indications of a violent recontre on the road, which have been considered as conclusive of the murder, actually occur within ten yards of one cottage, and a very short distance from another, the inmates of both of which heard the horse go by, but no other noise or struggle of any kind. From thence to the lime-kiln, where some have sapiently conjectured that his body was carried and consumed, must be at least a mile, and to have gone thither the murderers must have exposed themselves to the chance of observation the greater part of the way in the high public road from Chard to Crewkerne! And what was to be gained by all this painstaking? The hat, stick and horse remained. It was desirable, therefore, to raise an idea of his murder, and leave the matter to conjecture and exaggerations of the credulous that active pursuit after the offender might be paralyzed. This has answered accordingly. His friends affirmed that his circumstances were good, and that he had £1,000 after payment of his debts. This is notoriously untrue. Parties who have lent their names to his bills are threatened with proceedings upon them, and the remarkable celerity with which his property is already to be disposed of, does not augur well for those to whom he stands indebted. Stuckey was very active in collecting every shilling due to him immediately before his disappearance, and it is known that he took a considerable sum away with him. His account at the same time was overdrawn at the Bank, and his acceptances were becoming due daily. Why a meeting of his creditors has not been called, and the statement of his affairs submitted to them, is to us not mysterious, nor is it impenetrable to us, why those in the secret should still insist on his being murdered. Stuckey's parents lived very near the spot where it is said he was waylaid and killed; and it it is not a little remarkable that on that particular night he called on them after they had gone upstairs to bed, and took an affectionate leave of them, though he has been repeatedly known to pass the door without calling. So many frightful deeds of blood have occured in that part of the country of late, that we are sincerely glad in being able to assist in dissipating the alarm which, in our opinion, has been so falsely and infamously excited on this subject. The statement in some of the Papers that Stuckey's body had been found under a rick of brushwood, has no more truth in it than the numberless other tales afloat on the subject.'

The *Western Flying Post*, however, thundered to the defence of Mr Stuckey and wrote that there was not the least foundation for the supposition 'which has been so rashly urged by some contemporary journals of the unfortunate individual having absconded for the purpose of eluding his creditors.' A reward of £100 was offered for the apprehension and conviction of the supposed murderer but no one came forward. On the last day of August, the mystery of Simeon Stuckey's disappearance was finally solved and a sad Benjamin Hedbitch recorded in his journal that on the '31st August 1830 Farmer Harriss's reapers of Dinington found the body flat on the back in the wheat furrows among the standing corn. On examination his money £13.12.6 watch, and all he had on him when he left home was found in his pockets safe. I saw him in the furrow but the smell was beyond description. I think ten thousand people saw him before he was removed.'

On the morning of Tuesday 31 August, the local magistrates had met in the Windwhistle Inn and, after reviewing the results of the extensive interviews and inquiries carried out with the residents of the cottages in the vicinity of the supposed crime, they concluded that they were no nearer solving the builder's fate than they had been three weeks before. By early afternoon, however, everything had changed.

On Tuesday morning Edmund and Charles Harris were cutting wheat in a field at Dinnington which lay about a quarter of a mile from the spot where Mr Stuckey's hat and stick had been found and, as they cut into an area of flattened stalks, saw to their horror what they first thought to be a scarecrow but then proved to be a very decomposed corpse lying in a dip in the ground. Although the two reapers could not identify the body both were pretty certain that it was the missing builder and Charles Harris went hot-foot to his father, Joseph, the owner of the field, to report the awful find. Simeon Stuckey's friends in Chard were notified and at about four o'clock on the Tuesday afternoon, the coroner, Mr Caines, accompanied by a jury of 18 'respectable persons' arrived in the field and inspected the body over which Edmund Harris had stood constant guard. By now news of the discovery had spread throughout the district and a large crowd had gathered in the field to view the stinking corpse and speculate on the cause of its demise.

The coroner and his jury found the body of Simeon Stuckey, which was identified by a memorandum book discovered on the deceased, lying on its back on the side of the dip with the head at the bottom and the left arm thrown over it. Although the corpse was fully clothed, the coat was torn across the skirts, the waistcoat was unbuttoned and the shirt disordered as if the body had been dragged head first to its final resting place. Spurs were still on the boots and one had dug into the earth apparently in Mr Stuckey's death throes. The coroner ordered the body to be searched and cash amounting to £13.12s.6d. was found in the coat pockets and some half-penny pieces were scattered nearby; the dead man's watch was found still in its fob.

The corpse was in an advanced state of decomposition, the eyes had been pecked out by birds, it stank and 'presented a frightful appearance.' It was placed in a coffin and transported to the Red Lion Inn at Chard to await the postmortem examination and the inquest was adjourned until nine o'clock on the following morning.

On Wednesday, 1 September, the inquest resumed and first to give evidence were the two reapers who recounted the discovery of the body. The next witness was Charles Coles, a Chard cabinet maker, who had helped search the corpse and confirmed that it was that of

Mr Simeon Stuckey from the memorandum book and various other articles found in the dead man's pockets. Robert Perry, a labourer, who lived with his daughter Amy in Chillington alongside the road from Dinnington to Windwhistle, recounted that on the night of Monday, 9 August, he had gone to bed at nine o'clock and at about eleven o'clock he had heard a horse gallop by in the direction of Dinnington. Perry stated that he had left for work on the Tuesday morning at his usual time of five o'clock and, walking down the road to Dinnington, noticed that someone had been very sick near the gate to Mr Dowall's field which lay about 100 yards from his cottage. Some 140 yards further along at the bend in the lane Robert Perry found a gentleman's hat which he picked up and took back to his cottage instructing Amy to hand it over to anyone coming to claim the article. The witness stated that he did not notice any dirt on the hat and neither was it damaged. Amy Perry confirmed her father's account.

Susan Matthews was now sworn and stated that at about half past eight on the morning of 10 August she had been walking along the road to Dinnington. Near Dowell's gate she had seen the vomit and the blood and signs of the ground being torn and kicked up on the left-hand side. Some three feet from the blood stains she had discovered the stick and there were marks on the road as if something heavy had been dragged along it.

Margaret Lucy, the next witness, said that on the night of 9 August at about half past ten she had seen a man wearing a dark coat and light trousers sitting on a horse outside her cottage on the Dinnington road and he had asked her the way to Chard. When she told him the stranger had asked her to go with him and put him on the right road. Quickly declining the request Margaret Lucy hurried back into the security of her cottage and bolted the door. It was her opinion that the man was not tipsy. Her neighbour Joseph Woodland confirmed this testimony.

The next to give evidence was a master mason, Hugh Clark, who recollected that he was enjoying a pint of cider in the Windwhistle Inn on Monday 9 August when he saw Mr Stuckey, whom he knew by sight, enter at about half past six. The builder bought a pint of cider and sat down in the settle sharing the drink with the landlord. Clark stated that there were six or seven men drinking in the inn, one of whom told the witness that his name was Rowe and that he lived in Winsham. After about a quarter of an hour Mr Stuckey had risen to leave and taking out his purse paid for the cider with a sixpenny piece. Hugh Clark observed that the purse was made of yellow canvas and was about the size of a hen's egg which he thought indicated that it contained a fair quantity of money. Mr Stuckey had then left on his own and the witness did not see anyone follow him. Shortly after Mrs Biss, the landlord's wife came in followed by an old man wearing a short smock-frock and Clark went on to say that there was no discussion of Mr Stuckey following his departure. The witness left the inn at around half past seven and returned to his lodgings with the Russell family in nearby Cudworth. His landlord's wife, Mrs Russell, and Henry Down of Ilminster, who was whitewashing the house, were present and when he went to bed at about ten o'clock Henry Down was still there.

Mr Richard Sampson told the jury that on the Wednesday following Mr Stuckey's disappearance he had gone to the spot where the builder's hat had been found and some 20 yards along the road towards Dinnington he had seen marks on the banks and in the ditches on both sides as if several persons had been sitting there.

The next witness, William Smith of Chard, stated that on 9 August he had attended a funeral at Chillington Church and at about eight o'clock that evening, in company with his wife, had left Holcombe Lodge to return home. Between Holcombe Lodge and Windwhistle they had met a woman on Chillington Down who enquired whether she was on the right road for Lopen. Smith confirmed that she was and asked whether she was going to the village that evening. The woman replied that she was and that her journey was to see her son who lived at Lopen Mill. On the Chard side of Windwhistle, the Smiths met a wagon driven by 'old' Martin's wife carrying two female passengers. Next on the road was a man, whom William Smith did not recognise, walking towards Windwhistle and whom he described as wearing a light fustian jacket and being of middle-size. The Smiths then met an aquaintance, John Matthews, followed shortly after by another man they didn't know who enquired whether they had seen anyone answering the description of the first stranger going towards Crewkerne. William Smith confirmed that they had and he stated that the second stranger was of similar stature to the first and wore identical clothes. William Smith also deposed that the two men were not natives of Crewkerne.

The medical evidence was now given by Mr Eustace, a surgeon from Ilminster. He stated 'that on removing the hair from the head, with assistance of Mr Sylvester, he discovered two wounds on the right side; the one was smaller than the other; and on removing the scalp, a very considerable extravasion of blood was found between the scalp and the skull immediately connected with the wounds; on removing the skin under the largest wound, which was at the back of the head, a fracture was discovered to the extent of five inches and three-quarters extending to the base of the brain; from this proceeded several smaller fractures which would probably cause instant death; and their opinion also stated that most probably the fractures were inflicted by a blunt instrument.' Mr Eustace was of the opinion that 'the larger wound on the head would have caused a considerable flow of blood, and a discharge from the stomach.'

Mr Sylvester, the surgeon who had assisted at the postmortem, was then asked to testify and stated that he believed it would have been impossible for the deceased to have walked to the place where he was found after receiving such a wound.

Lawrence Biss, the landlord of the Windwhistle Inn, who was probably the most important witness, now took the stand. He stated that Mr Stuckey had come to his house on the Monday afternoon at about five o'clock. There were present at that time Mr Baker of Crickett, Richard Hutchings of Purtington, Joseph Cranton of Crickett, Hugh Clerk of Ilminster, John Balford, his son William Balford, and his brother Samuel from Butleigh. Mr Stuckey had a pint of cider which he had shared and had paid him for it. He stated that he had seen the purse, but did not know what was in it, or into which pocket Mr Stuckey had put it. The witness confirmed that the builder had not stopped for more than ten minutes and on parting had said that he would not wish the landlord good evening as he would see him again on his return. His customers had dispersed before seven o'clock and he recalled that Hugh Clark was the first to go and the Balfords and Joseph Cranton the last. His wife was not then at home and, although he had spent most of the time in the kitchen, when he was with his customers he could not recall any discussion of Mr Stuckey's money. Mrs Biss had returned home between eight and nine o'clock and Lady Bridport's coachman who had accompanied her did not stay long. The witness recollected that just before his wife returned a woman had called and asked the way to Lopen. At eight o'clock four men who had been helping the landlord thatch some hayricks and whom he named as James Morris, James Stanton, John Cranton and James Hill, finished their work and came into the inn for a meal. Hill and Cranton left after the meal but when Lawrence Biss went to bed at ten o'clock Morris and Stanton were still there. About ten minutes later the two remaining men left and Mrs Biss locked up and went to bed.

Lawrence Biss then recounted the events following his awakening by Norris, the Sheriff's officer, and the discovery of Mr Stuckey's riderless horse. Following the landlord's evidence 'two females were examined' and recalled that they were returning home along the road to Dinnington late on the Monday evening when they heard whistling as if several persons were in hiding and signalling to each other.

The inquest was then adjourned to the coming Friday morning at the Windwhistle Inn and although several other witnesses were called, no new evidence was given which could throw more light on the mystery of Mr Simeon Stuckey's violent end.

The jury were faced with a number of puzzling questions before they could arrive at a verdict. There was the difference in times when Mr Stuckey was said to have arrived at and left the Windwhistle Inn. Witness Hugh Clark stated that the builder arrived at half past six but the landlord gave the time as five o'clock, a difference of one and a half hours. Clark also stated that Mrs Biss arrived before he left at about half past seven but Lawrence Biss said that all the customers had left by seven o'clock before his wife came home between eight and nine o'clock. The jury do not seem to have questioned the discrepancies or, if they did, were satisfied that there was nothing sinister in them.

Robert Perry said that he heard the sound of a horse galloping towards Dinnington and away from the direction of Chillington Common. Who was riding so fast at eleven o'clock at night? Who was the stranger on horseback who had accosted Margaret Lucy? Who were the two strangers wearing identical clothes seen by Mr and Mrs William Smith on the Chard road? And was any money stolen or did the yellow purse seen by Lawrence Biss and Hugh Clark contain no more than the £13.12s.6d. At the time of the builder's disappearance his friend Benjamin Hebditch thought that he had £60 in cash on his person but perhaps this was only a rumour because no mention of such a large sum was made at the inquest.

The '18 respectable persons' of the jury could find no solution to the mystery and returned a verdict of wilful murder against some person or persons unknown.

The funeral of Mr Simeon Stuckey took place in Chard at four o'clock in the afternoon of Thursday 2 September. The procession left the Red Lion Inn, where the body had lain from the day of its discovery, and was carried by some of the builder's workmen to be interred in the precincts of the Independent Church where he had been a greatly respected worshipper for many years. Mrs Stuckey, accompanied by two female friends, followed in a chaise past the several thousand townspeople who lined the route to the Church.

The allegations made in the columns of the *Taunton Courier* of the reasons for Mr Stuckey's disappearance were still causing his friends much annoyance and the following letter appeared in the same edition of the *Western Flying Post* as the reports on the inquest and the builder's funeral.

Sir,

Perceiving an article in the *Taunton Courier* of the 25th ultimo, which so deeply reflects on the character of Mr Stuckey, and those friends of his who have taken an interest in his fate, I cannot suffer it to pass uncontradicted. It is stated in the *Courier* that 'there is neither murder or mystery in his fate': but what will the writer of this assertion say now that his murdered body is found? He further says, 'that it is desirable to raise the idea of his murder in order to prevent pursuit,' and 'that the parties who lent their names to his bills are threatened with proceedings upon them.' Let him name those parties if he can: but the fact is, such parties have no existence. With regard to the disposal of part of his property, so convinced were Mr S's fiends that nothing short of his death could have caused his disappearance, that they advised his widow to discontinue the business as soon as possible, and to dispose of his horses and farming stock immediately, which was done fourteen days after his disappearance. What could a woman, in her afflicted state, do with an extensive business (in which about thirty men were employed) but to dispose of it as soon as possible. Horses standing idle – cattle neglected – corn ripe for the sickle, – under these circumstances it was decided advisable to sell the whole of the farming stock to free the widow's mind as much as possible from perplexity and anxiety; and in due course to advertise the business and stock in trade to be disposed of either by auction or valuation. It is then said that 'Mr Stuckey had been previously actively engaged in collecting every shilling that was due to him, and that his account at the Bank was overdrawn, and his acceptances were becoming due daily.' The whole of this is incorrect. His account with the bank is most respectable and the last time it was balanced, he was indeed, debtor in the heavy amount of 18s.6d. At this moment the Bank is indebted to him for work which he has done.

Stratton was Mr S's native place; and he was never known to enter the village without calling on his parents but once, and at that time he was particularly occupied. On the 9th of August last he called as was his custom. His father was unwell in bed. Mr S went upstairs to see him, and remained a few minutes only because it was late. His father asked him if he had brought back a basket which he had sent him with some plums; to which Mr S replied he had not, but he was coming again to Stratton the next day or the following and he would then do so. This interview is magnified into 'taking an affectionate farewell of his parents; in a way,' too, 'which he had never done before.' Now, Sir, I challenge the writer of these statements to a proof of the facts asserted, if he have any.

I am, Sir, yours etc.,

A FRIEND OF THE LATE MR STUCKEY

The verdict of the inquest jury did not see the immediate closing of the inquiries into the murder and Mr Samuel Taunton, the Bow Street runner who had hunted the killer of Betty Trump seven years before in the wild Blackdown Hills, was reported to be in the neighbourhood on the lookout for a man strongly suspected of having committed the 'horrid deed.' The reward for the apprehension and conviction of the murderer or murderers was increased by public subscription to the huge sum of £500, equivalent to twenty years wages for an agricultural labourer.

Despite the Bow Street runner's efforts and the reward, the killer or killers of Mr Simeon Stuckey were never apprehended and the mystery of the builder's death was never solved.

Was it the case of a robbery which went horribly wrong, the assailants in blind panic fleeing without their booty, or was Mr Stuckey mistaken for someone else in the darkness of that August night and paid the penalty for being in the wrong place at the wrong time?

'HOW YOUR HAND DO SHAKE, GEORGE'

Just after seven o'clock on Wednesday evening, 28 March 1883, William Mullet was at home in his cottage in High Street, Henstridge, when someone knocked at his front door. On opening it he found George White standing on the step. His first thought was that there might be trouble in store because five months before his lodger, Clara White, had left her husband George after only a few weeks of marriage, and on the previous occasion he had called he had taken her out and given her a beating.

'Is Clara here?' was the enquiry, to which William Mullet cautiously replied that she had gone to the well in Furge Lane to fetch some water. George White then asked how Mullet was getting on in his new job as a ganger on the Somerset and Dorset Railway and whether he thought there would be any chance of him being employed as a labourer. William Mullet felt that there would be no work for him and the two men walked out into the High Street. After waiting for a few minutes, but with no sign of Clara, White bade good evening and strolled down the road towards Furge Lane.

Shortly after, Clara returned home and told William Mullet that her husband had asked her to go for a walk. She said that she had at first refused but as George had been so insistant she had reluctantly agreed. Taking off her shawl, Clara put on her jacket and left just before half past seven.

Fred Gould and Robert Garland were chatting outside the Henstridge Wesleyan Chapel when they saw George White sauntering down the High Street and as he passed he remarked, 'You seem busy.' A few minutes later he came back and taking Fred aside, asked if he could have a word with him in private. Fred, who had worked with White on the Inwood Estate, agreed and the two men went into the Chapel yard.

Once inside George White asked, ' Fred, will you do something for me?'

'Depends on what it is,' was the reply.

'I want you to pray for my soul.'

'George, you must pray for yourself but why do you ask me?'

'Because I mean to do for her tonight!' hissed White.

Alarmed by the vehemence, Fred asked who he was going to 'do'?

'My wife, and I've come down for the purpose,' was the reply.

Fred Gould then grabbed White by the front of his collar and pulled him forward exclaiming, 'George White, if you say that again I'll give you in charge of a policeman and I should be justified in doing it! If you do such a thing I'll be a witness against you!'

White only laughed back, 'I didn't mean it Fred but Clara bothers me so. She have written me four or five letters and I've come down to see her about it.'

Smelling beer on George White's breath, Fred Gould told him to go home and take himself to bed.

'I'll see her first and then I will,' was the reply.

As the two men returned through the Chapel gates Fred saw Clara standing nearby and he watched the couple walk off together down the road towards Henstridge Ash.

At about a quarter to eight, George and Clara White entered the Bird in Hand public house and George ordered a pint of beer. As he poured it, Ann Gulliford, the publican's wife, heard Clara remark, 'How your hand do shake, George. How you be wasting it, George.'

'Never mind', was the reply and no further words were spoken.

Later Ann Gulliford would recall that the couple stayed for less than ten minutes but during that time they sat side by side and seemed comfortable together sharing the beer.

At about eight o'clock Arthur Avis, a young wheelwright, and Elizabeth Tite, in company with Edwin Hann and Ellen Palmer, were walking home to Stalbridge from Templecombe. The night was very dark but as they reached the top of Yenston Hill they heard screams coming from somewhere up ahead towards Henstridge . At first they thought it was children playing but as Arthur and Elizabeth, who were about 150 yards in front of their friends, reached Inwood Lodge, the screaming took on a desperate tone and Elizabeth expressed her fear that something might be wrong. At that moment the figure of a woman appeared out of the darkness walking from the direction of Henstridge, but said nothing as she passed. Arthur reassured his partner that if anything was amiss the woman would have told them, but, sensing that everything was not quite right the couple quickened their pace.

The screams continued and Arthur became aware of the sound of blows. Suddenly, in the darkness, he could make out the figures of a man and woman struggling on the left hand side of the road. The woman was lying on the grass verge and just as the couple passed the man began kicking her. Arthur Avis walked across to the man, whom he did not recognise in the dark and took to be a tramp, and shouted at him to stop hurting the woman.

'It's not your business, this is my wife and I can do as I like with her!' was the reply and more kicks were administered.

Arthur shouted back to Edwin Hann to come and give him a hand as a woman was being attacked and seeing the woman on the ground as he ran up, Edwin called the man a drunken sot for beating her so.

At this, the man stopped kicking the woman and moved in a threatening way towards the four young people roaring, 'Who's drunk? Explain yourself and mind what you're saying or else you'll get it too. She's alright. She can walk if she likes!'

He returned to the woman who had managed to stand up only to be knocked down again and the kicking recommenced. Edwin Hann then shouted that he would go for the police and ran off towards Henstridge, whilst Arthur Avis began to throw stones at the man in an endeavour to distract his attention from his victim.

Sergeant Major Charles Stanbrook of the Blackmoor Vale Troop of Dorset Yeomanry, was an ex-regular soldier, and in company with James and John Brockway, was walking from Templecombe to Henstridge when he heard cries and shouts for help. He ran to find out was was happening and saw a young man with two young women standing at the side of the road and a few yards away he could make out the figure of another man standing over a woman lying on the ground. One of the young women shouted that the man was murdering his wife and at that moment the sergeant major saw the man kick the woman's head.

Charles Stanbrook's actions were swift. He stepped forward and, with one powerful blow from his walking stick, felled the man who was then secured by the two Brockways. The sergeant major knelt down beside the unconscious woman, but, as he raised her head to see if she was breathing, she died.

By now a number of people who lived in the area had arrived and the sergeant major took charge. He was told that the policeman had been called and so he sent the Inwood lodgekeeper into Henstridge for the doctor and John Brockway for a conveyance to take the dead woman to the village. A lantern was brought and the man was quickly identified as Charles White and the bloodstained corpse as his wife, Clara.

When Police Constable Culliford arrived breathless from Henstridge, he found about 20 people crowded around the body and a man being held by Sergeant Major Stanbrook and James Brockway. He identified the prisoner as George White and was told that the dead woman on the ground was his wife. After handcuffing White, the constable searched him and found a double-bladed clasp knife in the right hand pocket of his waistcoat. Having completed his search, Constable Culliford quickly examined the dead woman and noted that she was bleeding from her face and head. He then charged George White with the brutal and wilful murder of his wife and after the caution the prisoner replied, 'Yes, I done it.'

John Brockway now brought up a small cart and Clara'a battered body was placed in the back to be taken back to the lodgings she had left just over an hour before; Constable Culliford and his prisoner made their way to the Wincanton Police Station. The murder caused a sensation in the area and, as the news spread, people came from far and wide to see the bloodstains on the road where Clara White had been killed. George White was brought before the Wincanton magistrates during the following morning and after being formally charged was remanded in custody until the 2 April.

On Saturday, 31 March, the inquest on the body of Clara White was held in the crowded National Schoolroom in Henstridge. The coroner and the jury had viewed the body at William Mullet's house and then walked to the schoolroom where the examination of the witnesses began.

William Mullet was the first to give evidence, and told of the call by George White and the reluctance of Clara to go with him. The foreman of the jury asked the witness whether the deceased woman had been living 'a constant life as a married woman' during the time she had lodged with his family. 'Yes', Mullet replied, but the coroner put a stop to this possible line of enquiry and pointed out that such questions were not necessary as the jury's duty was to inquire into how the death had occurred and not why; what passed between the husband and his wife would be heard at any trial. Fred Gould kept his promise and testified on White's threats to 'do for her', and Ann Gulliford recounted the conversation in the Bird in Hand. Arthur Avis, Elizabeth Tite and Edwin Hann described the events on the road near Inwood Lodge and Sergeant Major Stanbrook told of his part in disabling and apprehending George White.

The mystery of the woman on the road was solved when Elizabeth Bulgin came to the stand. She said that she had been returning home to Yenston and recalled seeing a man standing by the side of the road near the spot where she had heard a murder had been committed. She did not know the man, who had wished her 'good night', and did not see a woman lying on the ground but, she pointed out, it had been a very dark night. Elizabeth Bulgin remembered passing the two couples near Inwood Lodge, but denied hearing any screams or cries for help, and then explained that she was a little deaf in one ear.

Police Constable Culliford recounted his actions at the scene of the murder and how, after sending for Dr Long to examine the dead woman, he had taken George White to Wincanton police station. There, in the presence of Superintendent Williams, White took off his blood-stained gaiters and boots, the knife was examined and found to be covered in blood and hair, and the prisoner's trousers and shirt cuffs were splashed with blood. There were gasps and exclamations from the public as the constable presented the articles for inspection by the jury. Constable Culliford stated that there was a long cut on White's forehead from the blow administered by Sergeant Major Stanbrook and this was bleeding freely when he was taken into custody.

Dr Robert Godolphin Long, medical practitioner of Stalbridge, stated that at about nine o'clock on the Wednesday evening he had been summoned to attend a woman in Henstridge. When he arrived at William Mullet's house, Clara White had just been brought in and he confirmed that she was quite dead. His preliminary examination revealed the head and face covered in cuts and bruises and these appeared to have been caused by some blunt instrument.

Dr Long stated that he had carried out a more careful examination on the following morning. He found a stab wound 5 inches long on the right side of Clara's neck which had severed the carotid artery and the jugular vein and there was a 3 inch stab wound on the left side. There was also a long abrasion across the throat as if an attempt had been made to cut it. The doctor found a large wound under Clara's left eye, the bones of the face were broken and there were cuts and bruises all over her face and head. Clara's lip was cut through on the left side and her hands were bruised and cut from her struggles to defend herself. The cuts and stabs could have been inflicted with the knife produced in evidence and in his opinion the blood and hair found on it were human. Dr Long had also examined the boots worn by White and believed the wounds on the deceased's head and face could have been caused by them.

He considered that the blows to the head were sufficient to kill Clara and the stab wound on the right side of her neck alone would have caused her death by the considerable haemorrhage which had occurred. After the coroner had summed up the case the jury retired for a very short time and returned a verdict of wilful murder against George White.

Clara White's funeral was held in Henstridge churchyard immediately after the inquest and a 'goodly number of women and children attended the service, some being very much impressed with the
solemn ceremony.'

George White appeared before the Wincanton magistrates on
Monday 2 April, when he was described as being an average looking
man of twenty-five years of age with red hair and sharp, ruddy
features. He had a somewhat sullen look and did not appear to feel
the seriousness of his position as he stood for the greater part of the
time with his arms folded watching the proceedings. The evidence
given at the inquest was repeated and on completion of the depositions George White was committed to Shepton Mallet prison to await
trial at the Spring Assizes in Taunton. On the 27 April 1883 George
was brought to the assizes and before the judge, Baron Huddleston,
he pleaded 'guilty, in a clear voice' to the indictment of having
wilfully and of malice aforethought murdered his wife Clara White
at Henstridge on 28 March. Baron Huddleston, however, was
anxious that the prisoner should fully appreciate the nature of the
guilty plea and the consequences which would inevitably follow his
conviction. The judge, after twice asking the prisoner if he fully
understood the charge and receiving his affirmation, called Mr Kitely,
the governor of the County Gaol, and following a private conversation, the governor went into the dock and took White to one of the
private rooms in the court. Here he explained the position in great
detail to George White but on returning to the dock and being asked
how he pleaded 'Guilty' was the reply.

Baron Huddleston then donned the black cap and sentenced
George White to death.

Later in the day, the judge called Sergeant Major Stanbrook and
told him that he wished to express publicly his sense of the courage
the soldier had shown in disarming George White compared with the
action of the two young men 'who from a strange presence of mind
and courage contented themselves in throwing stones at the person
who at that time was actually killing his wife.' In recognition of the
sergeant major's conduct, Baron Huddleston ordered that he should
receive a reward of £5.

A few minutes after eight o'clock on the morning of Monday 21
May 1883, the bell of the County Gaol at Taunton began to toll and
two men, George White, and Joseph Wedlake who was paying the
ultimate penalty for the mistaken killing of Mark Cox in a fit of jealousy at Winford, began their final walk to the scaffold. With arms
pinioned, they were placed on the drop, legs were strapped, white

caps drawn over their heads, ropes secured and Marwood, the public hangman, pulled the bolt sending both murderers into eternity. After hanging for an hour, the bodies were cut down and buried within the precincts of the gaol. It was George White's twenty-sixth birthday.

What then, were the demons which drove George White to beat and stab his wife to death on that dark March evening in 1883? There is a small clue in the question the foreman of the inquest jury put to William Mullet with whom Clara White lodged. It will be recalled that he asked if Clara had been living a 'constant life as a married woman', but this line of questioning had been stopped by the coroner as not relevant to their inquiries.

Then there was a report in the *Western Gazette* on 25 May 1883, stating that after the execution it had became known that a petition had been presented to the Home Secretary seeking a reprieve for George White and setting out details of 'some domestic matters of a painful nature hitherto withheld.'

In the Public Record Office at Kew there is a bundle of papers which perhaps provide the answer; they disclose the terrible truth. George White had contracted syphilis from Clara after they were married. Because George White had pleaded guilty at his trial, no jury had heard the case and this distressing fact was never told. There was also no petition as reported in the newspaper, but the rector of Henstridge, the Reverend Alexander Ainslie, wrote two urgent letters to the Home Secretary setting out the details of George White's illness and the causes. He explained that he had been abroad when the murder had been committed but on his return had been acquainted with the facts which he now communicated to the Home Secretary. The rector suggested that if this information had been given to a jury they would have made a recommendation for mercy. The letters were supported by Dr Scallon, of Milborne Port, who had been treating George White for the disease, who told how ill and depressed his patient had been for many months prior to the murder. In the minds of both men, there was no doubt that Clara had infected her husband who believed that he had married a woman of good health and moral character. It had soon transpired, however, that Clara White had led an extremely 'dissolute' pre-nuptial life.

The Home Secretary was not influenced by the efforts of the rector or the doctor and no reprieve was given. Can we imagine the hurt, the despair and the humiliation felt by George White, or the anger which raged in his fevered brain? If we can, then we know the demons which drove him to the gallows.

'YE THOUGHTLESS YOUTHS A WARNING TAKE'

It was the evening of Sunday 17 December, 1854, when two young labourers from Hinton St George, John Sealy and Will Eason, sauntered into the George Inn in Merriott and joined William Lewis who was already enjoying a pint of beer in the warmth of the tap-room. More drinks were bought and the three young men settled down to a convivial evening, no doubt looking forward to the Christmas festivities just over a week away.

Then Edmund Horner came into the tap-room and spoilt the evening. Horner immediately began to poke fun at William Lewis and boast about the black eye he had given him during a fight at the last harvest. He then offered to fight Lewis again for a sovereign and, the challenge being accepted, both men stripped off their jackets. However, before they could set about each other, wiser voices prevailed and after re-dressing, both sat down, seemingly the best of friends. The drinking recommenced and such was the newly-found camaraderie, that Edmund Horner borrowed sixpence from William Lewis to pay for a round of beer.

At about half past ten, the four not too sober young men, left the George and started to make their way home in the bright moonlight to Hinton St George.

John Sealy and Will Eason were some little distance in front of Horner and Lewis but after they had walked about a quarter of a mile raised voices came from behind. The two men were arguing again, and Horner was heard to threaten to punch Lewis, who in return threatened to 'hit the knife into thee!'

Sealy and Eason, fearing more trouble, hurried back to stop it but, as they did so, Edmund Horner could be seen with his hat and jacket off, squaring up, and the moonlight was gleaming on a knife being waved by William Lewis. Horner was seen to swing several wild blows and although one knocked off Lewis's hat, none caused any injury. Another punch was thrown and Lewis's hat was knocked from his head for a second time, but then Horner screamed to Eason, 'Will! the knife is in me!' and fell against him. Horner was holding his groin and trying to stop the blood which was spurting though his fingers and pouring down the legs of his trousers. Will Eason helped

51

him to a nearby gate but after supporting the injured man for a few minute, Edmund Horner suddenly fell backwards, moaned a little and died; the knife had severed a main artery. Horrified, Eason shouted that Edmund had been stabbed but Lewis retorted that he hadn't done it and even if he had, there was no hurt 'for the knife did not go in very far.'

Constable Rowsell of Merriott was called and, helped by William Mitchell who lived nearby, the body was carried back to the George. William Lewis was taken into custody but no knife was found on his person.

The following morning, Constable Rowsell returned to the scene of the stabbing, which was marked by two large pools of blood, and following a careful search of the road and ditches, found the blood stained knife. It was identified as belonging to William Lewis, who, on being cautioned said, 'I will never do any such thing anymore, I shouldn't then, only both of us were very tipsy.'

Lewis was committed for trial at the Somerset Spring Assizes of 1855 charged with the murder of Edmund Horner but the charge was subsequently reduced to manslaughter of which he was found guilty and sentenced to fifteen months hard labour. A weathered tomb stone in the churchyard of Hinton St George bears witness to that Sunday evening which began so quietly and ended so tragically and on it, Edmund Horner's epitaph warns of the dangers of breaking the Sabbath.

> Stabb'd by a fellow workmates hand
> A sad revengeful hate
> This stone a monument shall stand
> Of my untimely fate
> Ye thoughtless youths a warning take
> From sinners turn away
> God's Holy Word your guidance take
> And keep the Sabbath Day
> Prepare to me an early grave
> Trust in His blood who came to save

'WHAT A FOOL I'VE BEEN – I'VE NOT DONE IT YET'

Some people seem to be doomed, and thirty-four-year-old Albion Wadman of Wincanton was one such doomed person. His wife was in a lunatic asylum, two of his three young sons were ill in Wincanton Workhouse, his failing health and sight were preventing him from following his trade as a shoemaker, he was desperately poor and in the early morning of Tuesday 17 April 1883 he went to Spring Close with seven-year-old John, his eldest boy whom he loved dearly, and cut the child's throat.

Just before ten o'clock on that Tuesday morning, Police Sergeant David Smith was in his house at Wincanton police station when Albion Wadman covered in blood came to his door and asked to be taken into custody because 'I have killed my little boy. He is up at the top of the lane and you will find him in the field with a razor by his side.'

Superintendent Joseph Williams was working in his office when Sergeant Smith brought in the blood-stained and trembling Albion Wadman and reported that, 'this man says that he has killed his son at Spring Close.' He instructed the sergeant to call out Constable Scadding and then take Wadman to the place where he said the boy had been killed. The two police officers, led by the father, left the station and began to walk up the steep Conygar Lane towards Spring Close. Before they were half way up the lane, Superintendent Williams joined them, and, reaching the stile at the top, he was the first to climb over into the field. In the ditch on the left hand side of the the stile and near the footpath which led over the hill, lay the body of a young boy covered in blood. A closer inspection revealed that the child's throat had been cut and stuck in the bank by the body was an open razor.

Albion Wadman, who had been held at the stile by Constable Scadding, cried out, 'Let me come up! let me come up!' and on being allowed to see the child, wept, 'Is he dead? Is he dead?' The superintendent confirmed that the boy was dead and then cautioned and charged Albion Wadman with the murder of his son. Wadman was taken the 200 yards back to the police station and lodged in one of the cells; Sergeant Smith remained with the body.

Doctor James Colthurst, accompanied by Superintendent Williams, now arrived on the scene and examined the dead boy, He found the child lying on his back with his legs doubled up, the head thrown back and the throat cut from ear to ear. The doctor was shown the razor found next to the body and which, from the blood that stained it, was evidently the murder weapon. Following the doctor's examination the corpse was carried to the dead house at Wincanton workhouse to await inspection by the coroner and his jury.

On Wednesday afternoon, Albion Wadman was brought before the Wincanton magistrates. The prisoner was described as being small in stature, looked wretched and was constantly twitching his moustache in a nervous manner. His eyes were swollen and red from crying 'whilst his well-worn pocket handkerchief was saturated with tears.' The police and Doctor Colthurst gave evidence and were followed by two local witnesses who had seen and spoken to Wadman before the murder was committed, together with a witness to the prisoner's state of mind.

The first to enter the box was Frederick Tucker who said that he had seen Wadman and his son walking along Grant's Lane in the direction of Spring Close. He recalled the prisoner saying, 'Good morning Mr Tucker. Have you done gate hanging?' To this the witness had replied, ' Yes, and I'm around painting. I think it's going to rain.' Wadman had then said, 'I don't think it is going to be much and I'm going for a walk.'

Frederick Tucker watched the father and son walk away along the lane with the boy following his parent as he always did; there was nothing particular about the pair.

The next witness was Eliza Day, a neighbour of the prisoner in The Tithing where he lived. At about half past eight on Tuesday morning, she was standing at her garden gate when the prisoner and his son passed and the following conversation ensued.

Prisoner, 'Good morning'.

Witness, 'Good morning Mr Wadman'.

Prisoner, 'How are you this morning?'

Witness, 'Quite well thanks. How are you?'

Prisoner, 'Middling. T'is a nice morning. I'm going to pick some flowers for my little boy'.

Eliza Day recalled that the boy did not speak and the prisoner, despite being 'middling', seemed in low spirits.

Emma Steele, a married woman who lived near the police station, came forward to give evidence on the state of the prisoner's mind.

She said that in the winter the prisoner had repaired a pair of her boots and, when he had brought them back, she had invited him to stay and have some tea as she knew he was badly off. Albion Wadman had declined and so she had given him some cake which he had taken home for his boy. The prisoner had told her that he was in trouble about his boy who wouldn't listen to him and said that 'I shall have to do for him' or 'I shall do for him.' The witness had begged him not to say or think such things and pray to the Lord that he might be preserved from any such temptations. She had then told the prisoner to take his son to the workhouse as it would be better for him to give up the boy but he said that he did not wish to. It was well known that he was very proud of the lad and they went everywhere together. Emma Steele stated that she had mentioned the conversation to one of the prisoner's brothers.

Police Constable John Bailey testified that at about half past three on the Tuesday afternoon he was on duty in the cell when the prisoner suddenly began to weep and said. 'I have had this on my mind for the past three weeks and every morning when I woke something seemed to say to me, "What a fool I've been, I've not done it yet." I intended to do it before but couldn't get the chance.'

Albion Wadman was committed to the prison at Shepton Mallet to await trial at the Spring Assizes. The case caused a sensation in Wincanton and was said to have been the first murder committed in the town within the memory of the oldest inhabitant.

Albion Wadman was a native of the town. He was described as a quiet, steady man and at one time was a member of the Good Templars Lodge of total abstainers. His aged father was still alive and his several brothers were all shoemakers in Wincanton. Wadman was brought before Baron Huddleston, the judge presiding at the Assizes, in Taunton on Saturday 28 April 1883. He was undefended and, in a faltering voice, pleaded 'Guilty'. Before the case proceeded, however, Mr Kitley, the governor of the County Gaol, took the prisoner aside and, after a short conversation, Wadman returned to the dock and, bursting into tears, pleaded 'Not Guilty'.

The case for the prosecution was opened by Mr Hooper who outlined the events of the 17 April and the witnesses who had appeared in the magistrates' court recounted their evidence. The prosecution contended that the prisoner's actions had been deliberate and that he knew what he was doing. It would be the duty of the jury if satisfied that the mind of the prisoner at the time of the crime was such that he knew what he was doing was wrong, to find him guilty.

Doctor R. Wybrants was called and said that he had attended

Wadman for some three years and produced a certificate which he had issued in December 1880 to the effect that the prisoner was suffering from cerebral irritation which prevented him from following his trade and caused affection of the eyesight. Since then he had treated the prisoner for anaemia, or poorness of the blood, and therefore the brain would not be nourished sufficiently. The doctor had not known Wadman to suffer from any form of insanity but he believed he would be so affected that at times he would not know whether he would be doing right or wrong.

The medical officer of Shepton Mallet prison, Doctor James Hyatt, took the stand and stated that the prisoner had been under his supervision for a week and he had seen him daily. He thought the prisoner had a weak mind and when spoken to he cried. Also his mode of walking showed that there was a disease of the brain. Doctor Hyatt believed that the prisoner was so suffering that the slightest thing could throw his mind off balance and cause him to commit acts in which he could not distinguish right from wrong. Perhaps it was because Albion Wadman had no defence counsel that the concluding address by Mr Hooper to the jury was scrupulous in its objectivity. He said that if they thought the prisoner not accountable for his actions at the time he killed his son, they could find him not guilty on grounds of insanity, but if they were not satisfied on this point, then they must return a verdict of guilty, notwithstanding any feeling they might have for the prisoner.

Baron Huddleston, in his summing up, said there could be no other conclusion than that the prisoner had caused the death of his child and, in the eyes of the law, this was wilful murder. However, as well as being wise the law was humane and provided that the prisoner was not accountable for the act at the time he committed it, and the jury were of that opinion, it would be their duty to say that the prisoner was not guilty on grounds of insanity. The statement made by the prisoner in the cell at Wincanton showed that his mind had been impressed with the thought of murdering his child for some considerable time. The medical witnesses had also shown that the prisoner was suffering from mental disease which might, at times, take such a turn that he was likely to commit acts when he was unable to distinguish between right and wrong. The jury would be justified in accepting the evidence of experts in a case of insanity, but only so far as such evidence presented itself to their sense of right or wrong.

It took only a short time for the jury to return a verdict of 'Not Guilty on the ground of insanity', and Albion Wadman was ordered to be detained during Her Majesty's pleasure.

Why did Albion Wadman kill his beloved son? Perhaps the thought of losing him to the workhouse was more than he could bear and if he could no longer have the child then no one else should either. To plead guilty would almost certainly mean that he would be executed and perhaps his fevered mind told him that this was the only way he could be with his boy in heaven away from all the cares of the world for ever.

THE KILLING IN THE CLOVER FIELD

At about half past five in the late afternoon of Thursday 25 October 1838, the season's mowing ended on James Astens' farm at Kingsbury, Milborne Port. The mowing team of James Osmond, William Brake, John Newport and George Hamblyn, led by foreman, William Stacey, cut the last of the seed clover and began to walk back across the field to where they had left their jackets and flagons of strong ale. It was starting to drizzle and the light was beginning to fade.

Suddenly to everyone's surprise, James Osmond exclaimed, 'There I've done with thee!' and tossed his scythe over the hedge into the adjoining field. A few moments later the labourer scrambled after it and wrenching the blade from the handle threw the blade into the nearby stream and shouting, 'Take care!', hurled the handle back over the hedge.

By the time James Osmond rejoined his companions they had settled down to finish their day's bread and cheese and were lubricating their dry throats with the last of the strong ale supplied by Farmer Astens. Throwing down the handle of his scythe, Osmond looked around exclaiming, 'Where's my other scythe?' On being directed to the swathe of clover in which it lay, he walked across and without a word picked up the implement and threw it into the next field. Once again Osmond scrambled after it and tossed the scythe back over the hedge. Then he returned, and after detaching the blade, picked up a heavy stick and began hammering the metal and bending it until it broke in two.

Until now his companions had watched these antics in silence but when the foreman, William Stacey, called out, 'Why do you make such a fool? Come and sit down and have some ale', Osmond came over and picking up one of the flagons threw it away.

'That was a foolish thing to do!' exclaimed William Stacey to which Osmond retorted, 'Mind thy own business!' and, after a pause, 'I'll fight thee or anyone else for a sovereign!' Although William Stacey was by nature quiet and inoffensive, he was a large fellow and could look after himself, so when James Osmond repeated the challenge he accepted it.

'If that's thy temper I'll fight ye Osmond. I'm your man!' he cried and stripping off his shirt Stacey took a fighting stance with fists raised. In a flurry of arms and fists the two men set about each other and the first to fall was William Stacey who went down on one knee with blood pouring from his nose. William Brake helped him to his feet and, after wiping the blood away, Stacey waded into his opponent and hurled him to the ground. Osmond quickly recovered and the fight continued.

Suddenly, William Stacey spun around gripping his stomach and screamed, 'Farmer, I'm done. I'm a dead man. My bowels are come out!' and, as the wounded man sank to the ground and rolled onto his back, William Brake saw to his horror the glistening coils of intestines spilling from a great gash in the foreman's stomach.

Help was summoned from Milborne Port and about half an hour later, Surgeon William Best arrived on the scene. Working in the light of a lamp he struggled to treat the hideous wound and after some twenty minutes finally restored Stacey's intestines to their rightful place. Meanwhile a cart had been called and the mortally injured man was placed gently in the back and taken to his home. As the drama of the evening unfolded James Osmond had lurked nearby denying that he had hurt his opponent and made off without rendering any assistance.

William Stacey lingered in agony until the following evening when mercifully he passed away.

The inquest was held on Saturday evening, 27 October, at the King's Head inn, Milborne Port, and the jury returned a verdict of 'Wilful Murder by James Osmond.' The prisoner was then committed to Ilchester Gaol to await trial at the 1839 Lent Assizes.

Six months later, James Osmond stood before the judge, Baron Gurney, in the Assize court at Taunton charged with the 'Wilful Murder of William Stacey by beating and stabbing him.' Mr Kingslake for the prosecution outlined the events of 29 October and called his first witness, William Brake, one of the mowers, who told of the prisoner's strange behaviour and the subsequent fight. He stated that William Stacey and the prisoner had worked together all summer and on the day of the fight they had been on very good terms. William Brake then explained that he had pleaded with the foreman not to continue fighting after he had been knocked his knees but to no avail. The witness also revealed that he had seen the prisoner with a knife earlier in the afternoon of the fatal day but had not seen a weapon used during the fight. In conclusion William Brake did not think either man was the worse for drink.

Fellow mowers, George Hamlyn and John Newport, next took the stand and corroborated the evidence of the first witness. Surgeon William Best described how he had been called to the field where he had found William Stacey lying on his back with his 'bowels protruding on the ground' and how it had taken him twenty minutes 'to put them in.' He stated that as William Stacey was being taken home, another local surgeon, Mr John Barrett, had met the party and the two medical men had been forced to perform another operation on the way to replace the deceased's 'bowels' which the bumping of the cart had displaced again. The surgeon then described the nature of the injuries. There was a wound six inches long across the abdomen and 15 other cuts and stabs including a slash at the top of the thigh, another under the ribs, one down the neck, and a vicious cut across the face dividing the left nostril. A knife in the hands of a powerful man would have caused the wounds and the stab in the stomach, together with the great loss of blood, had been mortal.

Surgeon John Barrett told of his attendance on the deceased and confirmed the medical evidence of his colleague. He produced some notes he had taken down during William Stacey's final hours in which the dying man had indicated his belief that there was no malice between the two men prior to the fight.

William Case, a labourer employed by Farmer Astens, testified that on 13 December he had found a knife in the ditch about 20 yards from the scene of the fight and he had given it to his master. Farmer James Astens corroborated his employee's evidence and produced the knife which had been indentified as belonging to the prisoner. He also confirmed that he had supplied about 4 gallons of ale to his mowers on the day in question as part payment for their labour. Farmer Astens stated that he thought James Osmond to be a quiet, peaceful man.

Mr Jardine addressed the jury on behalf of the prisoner, and submitted that it was clear from the evidence before them that the prisoner had no malice towards the deceased and therefore the crime could be considered to be no more than manslaughter.

In his summing up, Baron Gurney stated that if the jury were of the opinion that the prisoner had intended to use the knife before the fight or if 'he had used it before his blood was heated' then he was guilty of the crime of murder; but if they thought that he had no idea of using the weapon until his blood 'had been heated in the contest', the crime amounted to manslaughter.

The jury did not send James Osmond to the gallows but found him guilty of the manslaughter of William Stacey and sentenced him to be transported for fourteen years. On 6 May 1839, Osmond left Ilchester Gaol for the prison hulk *York* at Gosport, on the first stage of his long journey to the life of a convict in Australia.

There remain some questions which were not answered at the inquest or the trial because the prisoner was never asked to explain them. Why did James Osmond act in such an odd manner by throwing away his scythes and breaking them? Why did the two men, apparently on very good terms, fight in such a savage way? And why did James Osmond use a knife? Perhaps the answer is quite simple. After drinking nearly a gallon of strong ale each during the day, the two men were not, despite William Brake's evidence, very sober, and as an old saying puts it, 'when the beer's in the wits out.'

THE SLAYING ON SANDPIT HILL

Charles Davis and his two young ladyfriends were not relishing the thought of the 2 mile walk back to Langport from Curry Rivel that blustery late evening of Friday 6 March 1835. It was now well after ten o'clock and, as the trio passed the Bell Inn, they were overtaken by Mr John Harvey driving in his light cart. Harvey, a prosperous plumber and glazier, was returning home to Langport following the completion of business in Curry Rivel and the purchase of some cider.

As the plumber drew alongside, Charles Davis wished him good-night and then asked whether he would take the two girls back to Langport. John Harvey declined the request and, slapping the reins of his horse, disappeared into the darkness; he had just made the biggest mistake of his life.

The three young people now fell in with a crowd of friends and as they chatted and joked all thoughts of the walk to Langport were forgotten and an hour had passed before they finally set out for home.

It was just before midnight when Charles Davis and the girls reached Sandpit Hill, half way between Curry Rivel and Langport, and to their surprise they found John Harvey's horse standing across the road and the cart backed against the bank. There was no sign of the plumber but as Charles walked around the horse he could just make out a dark form lying on the ground. Assuming this to be John Harvey and that he had been drinking and had fallen out of the cart, Charles Davis called out to the recumbent plumber to get up. After receiving no response, and believing that the man was drunk and help would be needed to get him back into his cart, the three youngsters hurried on to the turnpike cottage about a quarter of a mile down the road. A lantern was lit and, accompanied by the grumbling gatekeeper, Charles Davis returned to Sandpit Hill where, in the wavering light, the man he thought drunk was seen to be cruelly battered and very dead. John Harvey was sprawled on his back with his clothing in disarray and his trouser pockets turned inside out. There was no doubting that the man was dead; his head was a bloody mess and the lower jaw so badly shattered that there were teeth scattered near the body. Leaving the gatekeeper to guard the corpse, Charles Davis raced to Langport where he raised the alarm at the New Inn and then went on to break the dreadful news to John Harvey's widow.

The plumber's body was carried to the New Inn but, as the coroner, Mr Richard Caines, was away on business, the inquest had to be delayed until the coming Monday.

In the meantime a killer or killers were on the loose and Mr Vincent Stuckey and Mr T.B. Uttermare, the local magistrates, aided by a number of prominent residents, set about hunting the perpetrators of the horrid crime and the assistance of the Taunton police officer, Mr Pomeroy, was secured.

On Saturday morning enquiries were made along the road from Curry Rivel to Langport and Mrs Elizabeth Cottle, a wealthy widow who lived in Portfield House some 200 yards north of the main road, came forward with a vital clue. She recounted that on the Friday evening she had gone to bed at about ten o'clock and that some time between ten-thirty and eleven o'clock, she had heard a disturbance on Sandpit Hill. Although this was a quarter of a mile away, the sound had carried well on the strong south-westerly wind. Mrs Cottle had called her servant to open the bedroom window but by the time this was done the noise had ceased. However, not long after, the widow heard voices in the lane outside her house followed by the sound of a splash as something was thrown into the nearby pond. The murder weapon had not been found and as this information looked more than promising, arrangements were made to drain the pond as soon as possible.

During Saturday's hue and cry, several men were taken in for questioning; one was a workman employed by the murdered plumber by the name of John Cothard from Muchelney and another was Samuel Tucker, a labourer from Huish Episcopi. Both men were released without charge but the record is silent on the reason for their arrests.

On Saturday morning, John Abrahams, still shocked by the murder of his employer, was in the plumber's workshop when John Hoare, one of the late John Harvey's apprentices, came in and asked if the soldering iron he had been using on Friday had been found. This was the first Abrahams knew of the iron being missing but thought no more of it when the apprentice left.

The fate of the soldering iron was brought back to John Abrahams' attention when on Sunday afternoon John Hoare had come back again asking if the iron had been found. Hoare thought the disappearance to be a great mystery but, when Abrahams wondered whether John Harvey had been carrying the iron in the cart and it might have been used to kill him, the apprentice told him vehemently not to make 'a bother about it' and left in a hurry.

The pond near Portfield House was finally drained during the Sunday afternoon and local shopkeeper, Arthur Stuckey, who had supervised the cold and muddy operation, was rewarded by the discovery of a large soldering iron which, despite its immersion, still retained some smears of blood and hair. One of the searchers was the apprentice, John Hoare, who identified the iron as belonging to his master; it was quickly confirmed that the hair matched that of the deceased plumber.

On Monday morning, 9 March, the inquest was opened by Mr Caines at the New Inn, where the body was viewed by the jury of 17 'respectable inhabitants', and then adjourned to the more commodious Guildhall. The jury sat through the afternoon and into the early evening considering the events of the previous two days which were continuing to unfold on an hourly basis. Several more men had been taken into custody during Monday morning and two of them were becoming the prime suspects.

Mr Caines adjourned the inquest until ten o'clock the next morning and the inquiry had been proceeding for less than half and hour when one of the magistrates, Mr Vincent Stuckey, entered the room and made a sensational announcement. A confession to the murder was being made by a person in custody and so the coroner immediately adjourned the inquest again.

Mr Caines and his jury next assembled at ten o'clock on Wednesday 11 March and the Guildhall was packed with spectators as two men were brought into the room. They were readily identified as nineteen-year-old cousins, John Hoare and William Howe, both of whom were appprentices to the murdered plumber.

The young men had been taken in for questioning on the previous Monday and had readily confessed to the murder and robbing of John Harvey. Hoare had implicated a man named Nichols in the killing but this part of the confession was quickly retracted as being a complete fabrication. The prisoners admitted stealing four sovereigns, a small diamond and some bills of sale and told where these articles could be found. A sovereign was recovered from under one of the bedposts in William Howe's bedroom and two sovereigns, the diamond, and the bills of account were dug up in Hoare's father's garden; Hoare had spent the fourth sovereign taken in the robbery.

The inquest jury, having heard the confessions, returned a verdict of 'Wilful Murder against John Hoare and William Howe', and the two prisoners were committed to Ilchester Gaol to await trial at the Somerset Lent Assizes.

At nine o'clock on the morning of Friday 3 April 1835 before Mr Justice Pattison, John Hoare was charged with 'having on the 6th of March, feloniously, maliciously, and with malice aforethought, with the right hand striking John Harvey, with a soldering iron, on the left ear, and giving him a mortal wound; and the said William Howe, for aiding and abetting the same.'

After hearing supporting evidence from various witnesses the prisoners' confessions were read to the jury and the story of the fatal evening unfolded.

William Howe was nursing a grudge. A week before the murder he had been sacked by John Harvey and the plumber had then refused to pay his former apprentice for work carried out before his dismissal. Howe's sense of grievance was encouraged by his cousin and fellow apprentice, John 'Banker' Hoare, and the two decided that if they could not get the money by fair means, then foul would do. It seemed that two previous attempts to obtain the money had come to nothing and hearing that John Harvey would be going to Curry Rivel on the Friday evening a plan was hatched to waylay him on his way home.

Hoare and Howe met at the Angel in Langport early that evening and, to steady their nerves, smoked a pipe of tobacco and downed about two quarts of beer and gin. Thus refreshed, they walked to Mr Harvey's house to enquire when he was expected back and having been told that he would not be long, Mrs Harvey asked Hoare to stay and stable the horse on her husband's return. Explaining that he had to meet someone Hoare excused himself and slipped into the plumber's workshop where, in addition to collecting his personal tools, he took the heavy soldering iron he had been using that afternoon. The two young men then went back to Hoare's home where they had supper and, telling his mother that they were going to meet Mr Harvey, the pair set out on their desperate venture.

The sound of the horse and cart could be heard on the wind long before the two cousins could see their victim. The plan was simple. Howe would grab the horse's head and Hoare would – do what? It is probable that neither really knew what they were going to do, but do something they would!

As John Harvey drew alongside, Hoare called out that he had come to meet him but puzzled, the plumber enquired why, and whether his wife was angry at his being late? The words were scarcely out of his mouth when Hoare sprang onto the cart and dealt him a fearful blow on the head with the soldering iron. The plumber fell forward onto his horse's back and then to the ground. Howe had held the animal steady but after turning it across the road, he fled into an adjoining field where he crouched trembling with fear at the violence of the past few moments. Hoare jumped down from the cart, but as he began to turn out his master's pockets, the plumber regained consciousness and called out, 'Banker, Banker, dont'y, dont'y!' – but 'Banker' did, and he proceeded to batter John Harvey into oblivion with the soldering iron. Howe, having regained his composure, rejoined his cousin but was horrified to see the beating starting again. 'For God's sake stop!' he cried, 'I can't bear to see it!' but Hoare continued, raging that John Harvey would 'not come to again.'

At last the beating stopped and completing the rifling of their victim's pockets, the cousins ran from the scene across the fields towards Portfield House where Hoare washed the blood from his hands in a waterfilled ditch and threw the iron into the pond. After sharing the meagre proceeds from the robbery both men retraced their steps to Langport and Hoare called back to Mr Harvey's to enquire if he had returned!

With the confessions read and their guilt established, the jury came quickly to a guilty verdict and after donning the black cap, Mr Justice Pattison sentenced the two men to death with the following words: 'John Hoare and William Howe, you have been found guilty on the clearest evidence, and indeed upon your own confessions, of a most foul and atrocious murder. It appears that you John Hoare, were the apprentice of the deceased person, Mr Harvey; and so far as I can find, there seems to have been no quarrel between you and him, therefore what motive you could have for committing this foul crime, remains in your own breast, whether it was done merely for the purpose of robbing him, or some vengeful motive, you alone and God can tell, for no man but yourself knows; but there is not the slightest doubt, both from the evidence and your own confession that you did strike him on the head with that instrument, and kill him, and that you must have gone out with the sole intention of so doing. With respect to you William Howe, it appears that there was a quarrel, and that you had been turned away; I do not know that you used any vengeful observations, but you had been turned out of his service. You laid in wait for Mr Harvey in the road; you could not possibly be ignorant of the object the other person had in view; you knew before that he had taken the weapon, which could only be intended for the perpetration of murder, and you had also some of the money of which he was robbed. There cannot be the slightest doubt that you must have gone out that evening with an intention of robbing, if not murder, and in the course of robbing him this foul murder was committed. In the eye of man, and according to the law of this land, you are equally guilty with Hoare. There can be no hope of mercy for either of you in this world and it is an offence which human law cannot pass over, neither can those who have the administration of the law in any case of murder, clearly proved, hold out any hopes of mercy. I tell you distinctly and plainly your time is limited in this world to next Monday and I therefore beg and beseech you to make the best possible use of you time in endeavouring to obtain pardon hereafter.'

After delivering some more strictures on their future conduct in the few days left, Mr Justice Pattison sentenced them to be hanged on the next Monday, 6 April, and their bodies buried within the precincts of Ilchester Gaol. The condemned men were taken from the dock with Hoare continuing to show the indifference he had evinced during the trial, but William Howe was badly distressed, hiding his face in a large handkerchief.

At eleven o'clock on the Monday morning, John Hoare and William Howe made their last public appearance before a large jeering crowd in front of Ilchester Gaol. Howe was very affected by the terror of the moment and even Hoare's apparent indifference collapsed when the rope was put around his neck. Both were in tears as they awaited their 'launch into eternity' but at least one spectator's indignation was aroused when instead of Hoare dropping his handkerchief as the signal for the trap to fall, he threw it from him with 'insolent obduracy of heart, and died amidst the universal execration of the multitude.'

The *Taunton Courier* recorded that, 'Hoare, young as he was, exhibited every characteristic of hardened brutality. At the Inn where he was lodged immediately on being taken to prison, he observed to those around him with impudent indifference to his situation, 'Come gentlemen, I think you ought to subscribe around, and treat me with some beer.'

Mr Justice Pattison was puzzled by the apparent wanton killing of John Harvey and could give no explanation why the attack took place. The confessions give no satisfactory reason and perhaps neither man could rationalise the motives which led them to kill on a windy March night and which brought them to the gallows one month later in front of Ilchester Gaol.

SUFFER THE LITTLE CHILDREN

During the reigns of Queen Victoria and her son Edward VII, 'baby farmers' could be found in towns and cities across the land. Women were paid fees or expenses to take into their homes the 'unwanted' babies of poor servant girls and other unmarried women who were unable, or unwilling, to look after their offspring. Many of these women were good and kind and the children lived with them for years until they could make their own way in the the world or could return to their mothers. But some were killers, and the name 'baby farmer' became associated through the pages of the popular press with sinister women lurking in dark houses into which children were taken never to reappear. There were two notorious cases of child-killing baby farmers; the first in 1896 when Amelia Dyer was executed for the murder of four-month-old Doris Marman, and the second in 1903 when the first women to be hanged in Holloway Prison were the murderous baby farmers, Annie Walters and Amelia Sach.

However, these were but the visible tip of the iceberg and no one will ever know how many 'unwanted' babies passed away by design or otherwise. The government was not unaware of the problem and legislation was enacted from time to time in an endeavour to prevent the abuse of the innocents. One Act of Parliament required a coroner to hold an inquest on the death of all illegitimate children who died under what might be considered unusual circumstances and one such case aroused much concern in Yeovil in the autumn of 1874.

Emma Pople's short life of fifteen weeks ended at noon on Saturday 19 September 1874, at the home of Mrs Caroline Fooks in Park Street, and on the following Thursday morning an inquest into her death was opened at the Globe Inn before the deputy coroner, Dr E.C. Garland, and his jury.

The first witness to be called was Mrs Caroline Fooks who said that she was a widow and recounted that early in June that year a young woman, who called herself Elizabeth Pople, had called at her house looking for lodgings. She was a stranger and explained that she had come to Yeovil for the birth of her baby and Mrs Fooks had been recommended as a good home for the confinement. The young woman would not tell where she came from, but did say that she was a servant. Mrs Fooks went on to say that a few days after she arrived, Elizabeth Pople gave birth to a baby girl who was named Emma and registered on 7 June. Shortly after the baby was born, a post office order for £8 was paid to Mrs Fooks by a man called Haggett from Shepton Mallet, and this was followed by a weekly payment of eight shillings.

Elizabeth Pople had left Yeovil about a fortnight after Emma's birth and had not been seen since. Following the death of the baby a man, unknown to the witness, had called and paid the £5 doctor's bill and funeral expenses. Mrs Fooks pointed out that she did not advertise that she took in and cared for children and reminded the jury that Elizabeth Pople had come to her by recommendation. She confirmed that a single woman had a confinement in her home about three years ago but the child was still living with her and she had received £30 to care for it for twelve years. Although this baby had been ill for several months it was now quite well.

Caroline Fooks then described the final illness of Emma Pople. She said that the child had been sickly from birth and since that time had been under the care of Mr Powell, the assistant of Dr Colmer. The baby had been taken ill in the morning of Saturday 19 September and had died at noon after suffering severe diarrhoea and convulsions. Mrs Fooks said that she had fed the baby on arrowroot, milk and wine and had never been told that this was wrong.

The next witness was Mrs Fooks' daughter, Louisa, who corroborated her mother's statements and said that the child had always been sickly. Her mother had been nursing Emma on the Saturday morning when she had been taken ill and gone into convulsions. Mr Powell had been called but could not save the baby which had died at noon. Mr Powell had given her the death certificate which she took to Mr Whitby, the registrar of births and deaths, and he had registered the child's death without comment.

At this point, Dr Garland, the deputy coroner, intervened and told the jury that the inquest was being held for two reasons. Firstly he was instructed by law to hold inquests on the deaths of illegitimate children who died under peculiar circumstances; and secondly, the death certificate in this case was illegal because it had not been signed by a qualified medical man. He had sent the certificate to the Registrar General for his decision and in reply had been informed that such certificates were disgraceful and illegal. The deputy coroner went on to say that this case was of a doubtful character and in the absence of proper medical evidence, the jury could not tell the cause of the child's death. Because Mr Powell, 'the medical attendant', was not a qualified medical practitioner he could not be called to give such evidence.

The deputy coroner stated that, in these most unsatisfactory circumstances, he had no alternative but to adjourn the inquest and order the post mortem examination of the child to establish the cause of death. The inquest resumed on Monday morning, 28 September, when the deputy coroner called Mr T. Powell, Dr Colmer's assistant, to give evidence on his actions when the baby died. The assistant confirmed that he had no medical qualifications and that he had signed the death certificate. Mr Powell went on to say, however, that from the beginning he had attended the child jointly with Dr Colmer but had treated Emma alone during her last illness. He had been present at the child's birth and confirmed that it had been sickly throughout its short life.

Mr Powell went on to say that he had made out death certificates in the absence of Dr Colmer and only recently had given one to a woman called Bidman for a premature still birth at a house in Stars Lane. When he gave such certificates, he wrote 'pro T.P.' but could not recall ever signing a certificate in Dr Colmer's name. After being warned by the deputy coroner that this statement could be checked because copies of the certificates could be obtained, the witness stood down.

Dr W.F. Tomkyns, who had carried out the post mortem, was the next and last witness. He testified that there were no signs of violence on the child's body and it was fairly nourished. All the internal organs which he had examined were healthy except the bowels, which were slightly congested. His examination of the brain, however, had showed much congestion and this could have been the cause of the convulsions and death. In the doctor's opinion the child died naturally but it would have had a much better chance of survival if it had been suckled at the mother's breast. He considered that children who were dry-nursed were frequently fed with improper food and this could cause an irritation of the stomach, followed by chronic diarrhoea and a fatal affection of the brain.

The deputy coroner then summed up and stated that Dr Tomkyn's evidence confirmed that Emma Pople had died from natural causes. However, the jury had heard what Mrs Fooks had said about the way she was paid for looking after children and there was the possibility of a premium being paid for the child to be deliberately neglected. Therefore cases, such as the one before them at this inquest, were bound to raise suspicions. He regretted that Dr Colmer had not thought it worth his while to see the child when it died so that a proper certificate could have been given, thus avoiding the necessity to hold this inquest.

Dr Colmer, who was present during this part of the inquest, was stung by these comments and although he sought to intervene he was ordered to remain silent by the deputy coroner. Continuing with his summing up, Dr Garland stated that this was not the first case of this kind they had heard about in Yeovil. He referred in particular to that mentioned by Mr Powell where a young girl had come to a 'house of ill-fame' in Stars Lane and given birth to a child. The child had been buried on the same day and the girl had left the town some two or three days later. In such cases, the registrar of births and deaths had the duty to return death as 'not certified', and the coroner would then decide whether there should be an inquest. If such cases were not dealt with properly and went unchallenged, he believed there would be little chance of stopping 'a certain class of crime'. Unqualified people had no right to give death certificates and, with a smile, the deputy coroner suggested that if this was the case his groom might as well be asked to sign them

The jury, after listening intently to the words of Dr Garland, returned a verdict of 'Death from Natural Causes' on Emma Pople. However, the verdict on the unfortunate child raised further questions and dark suspicions. Dr Colmer, angered by the comments of the deputy coroner, turned to the pages of the *Western Gazette* to state his case.

On 9 October the following letter appeared:

To the Editor
  Sir, The deputy coroner at the inquest of Emma Pople stated his surprise that, when Dr Colmer knew the child to be sickly from birth, he did not see her. My object in writing is to let the public know I did see the child on more than one or two occasions in my surgery; but Mr Deputy, although I was present at the adjourned inquest, deemed it proper not to ask me the question, or allow me to contradict the statement he made without having recourse to the newspapers. The certificate of death, of which Dr Garland complains, was signed in my absence by my assistant who had visited the child during the last few days of her illness and who considered the child better, and probably likely to recover, as she had done before, had convulsions not supervened, which, I will venture to state, cannot always be foreseen, even by our learned Deputy. I may

also state that I am not the only practitioner who sends an unregistered assistant to attend cases. I know of at least one other, who sends his young and inexperienced pupil to visit his pauper patients, which is strictly forbidden by the Poor Law Board.

Likewise, in the same edition, the assistant Mr Powell penned a stinging attack on Dr Garland, the deputy coroner, and hinted at some dark goings on by that official. He referred to the case of an infant death at East Coker and enquired why Dr Garland had dispensed with the company of the nurse when he had undertaken the post mortem. Mr Powell went on to suggest that as Dr Garland wished the public to believe that he was a strong enemy of secrecy or anything which looked like 'baby farming', perhaps he would, if he knew the facts, inform, in his public capacity, the twelve gentlemen who comprised the inquest jury, who the infant was which had been taken in a four-wheeled carriage to a house in Huish some eighteen months ago, and which 'chose to die some some few hours after its arrival.' He felt sure 'it would be edifying for the public to know who the father was, who the mother, and whether legitimate, and why the little thing should so soon have felt disposed to quit the town and its troublesome and prying neighbours.'

The correspondence was now warming up, and 'An Inhabitant' entered the fray, this time in the columns of the *Pulmans Weekly News* of 13 October and made some serious allegations:

Sir

It is quite time somebody interfered to find out the cause of such high mortality amongst illegitimate children. To arrive at this it is necessary and even advisable that the strictest enquiries should be instituted on all deaths of such. From the evidence adduced at the inquest it is evident that the death would have been a pecuniary gain to the 'Farmer'. Should this be?

That the deaths of illegitimate children in Yeovil are very high can be proved by the Registrar. Cases have been known where single women have gone to the town for the express purpose of being confined and, upon enquiry, a short time after, the child is invariably found to have died. Of what? Not poison, perhaps worse – either neglect, starvation, or the mismanagement which is not punishable and therefore chiefly relied on to effect the purpose. That coroner's enquiries have done good service in Yeovil cannot be denied. It is not many years ago that an establishment existed where young women were accommodated. I remember Inquests being held on 2 infant children of the same woman, who had come there to be accommodated. Exposure routed the company. Now, it seems, an attempt is being made to establish others, but with what success remains to be seen.

Mr Powell continued with the mystery of the Huish baby and on the 23 October he wrote in the *Western Gazette*:

Sir, As the curiosity of the public has been much aroused by my remark in your impression of the 9th inst. about the Huish baby, I will, in justice to others, lay before your readers the true and unvarnished history as told to me.

At the untimely hour of 4 am on May 2nd, 1873, a registered medical practitioner called out of their comfortable bed a Mr and Mrs_____ , residing in Huish and wished them to take charge of a new born infant, which they agreed to do and which was sent to them at eight o'clock, simply wrapped in one old article and a shawl. (Surely common decency and ordinary care for its life would have suggested its being dressed previous to removal from one place to another.) The child died within the next 48 hours, and a certain medical gentleman furnished the people in question with a small sum of money and an order for the Cemetery Keeper for the interment of this 'male child.' The Cemetery man refused to receive the body unless the scrap of paper had first passed the legal ordeal of being registered. This registered medical man, therefore, felt it necessary to seek the assistance of the Registrar; and after certifying the cause of death and signing the official book, he secured the necessary order for the interment of the 'male child.' I am only surprised that, after manifesting so much interest in the case, he should have forgotten where it died as to make the mistake of saying Park Street instead of Huish.

There are one or two questions involved in this transaction which probably some of your readers may answer. Was there not great necessity for an enquiry into the cause of death of this poor 'male child' of 'So and So' (I am anxious not to have the finger of scorn pointed at the unhappy mother). Might not the careless way in which in his early hours he was removed have, to a certain extent, accelerated his end? And were there not

73

strong grounds for a most stringent enquiry by the coroner as to whether there was any blame attached to anybody, or if there was anything like baby farming in the case? No doubt, had this case happened elsewhere, the public would have been made fully acquainted with the father and mother, and whether this 'male child' of _____ was legitimate or not.

There was no doubt against whom these allegations were made, and on 13 November, Dr Garland responded:

To the Editor of the *Western Gazette*
Sir, So long as Mr Powell and the anonymous clique of correspondents restricted themselves to the attempt to asperse my character, I made no comment; but as I see by a letter which appeared in your last issue an endeavour is made by implication to honour another in a like manner, I take this opportunity of stating that I attended (as is well known) a child placed by my professional advice under the care of a thoroughly competent married woman (who has acted as a nurse), and that I knew PERSONALLY, every possible care and attention was paid to the same by her, which perfectly justified me in granting the usual information given in such cases, which I did in my private capacity as a legally qualified registered practitioner who alone can furnish such.

'A Looker On' had a say on 27 November:

To the Editor
Dear Sir, It struck me, on reading the certificate given by Dr Garland in the baby farming case mentioned in your last paper, that 'inanation' was a strange term to use as indicating the cause of death. On referring to the dictionary for the strict meaning of the word, I find it given as 'Emptiness, exhaustion from want of food.'
Is the cause of death in accordance with the idea that the poor baby had proper attention, as stated by him?

'A Looker On', who ever he or she might have been, obviously had knowledge of the name of the baby which had died at Huish and had access to the register of deaths and was endeavouring to stoke the flames of a possible scandal. The author's researches have established that the child was a boy born on 1 May 1873 and the mother was Catherine Creed; the registrar entered Park Street as the place of birth. On 3 May, the death of the child is registered as a 'Boy', the son of Catherine Creed, servant, the place of death is Park Street, and the cause certified as 'Inanation.' The register of burials of the Yeovil Cemetery records that the infant child of Catherine Creed who died, aged two days, in Huish, was buried on 3 May 1873 without a ceremony of committal and lies in unmarked grave B.1707.

Dr Garland made no further forays into the columns of the local press, but Mr Powell then requested Dr Wybrants, the coroner for the Southern Division of Somerset, to open the 'Huish'case, but this was refused on the grounds that the law did not allow him to hold an inquest eighteen months after death. After this rebuttal, the affair spluttered to a close.

Without doubt there was a strong feeling of unease in Yeovil at the deaths of babies, both legitimate and illegitimate, during the mid-1870s, and a case of twins being allegedly starved to death did not help to calm matters.

In January 1875 the twin infant daughters of Louisa Maniford died in suspicious circumstances at their home in South Street, Yeovil. A post mortem carried out by Dr Colmer on the two children, one of whom was described as 'looking like a dried-up dwarf', and the other 'like an Egyptian mummy'revealed that the five week old infants had no traces of food in their systems and there was no sign of disease. Although all but one witness at the inquest stated that Louisa Maniford had cared for the twins, and Mrs Clements, her mother, had declared that 'Queen Victoria's children could not had been better cared for', there were suspicions that all was not quite right. The jury became even more concerned when they were told that at thirty-one years of age Louisa had already given birth to ten children of whom seven had died, all in infancy. The first was found dead by her side in bed when fourteen days old and an inquest had been held. There was no enquiry into the death of the second at fifteen days, as Dr Colmer had been in attendance. Dr Garland had attended the third which he had said was 'in decline', and the team of Dr Colmer and his assistant, Mr Powell, had treated the fourth, which passed away at four months. The fifth managed to survive for nine months before it declined and died, Dr Aldridge being in attendance on this occasion. Deaths six and seven were the subject of inquests.

With the record of fatalities in the household, even with local qualified medical men in attendance, the jury returned a verdict of 'death by starvation.'

Louisa Maniford appeared at the Assizes in the following April, charged with causing the deaths of her two infant children, but the story which unfolded was not one of a woman with murder in mind, but one of an inadequate mother facing an almost impossible situation. She lived in a house overcrowded and barely better than a hovel; her husband earned between 16 and 18 shillings a week in one of the town's leather dressing yards and was 'given to drinking', the contemporary euphemism for hard drinking, so there was little cash to spare for the home and family. Louisa had little idea of proper infant care or feeding and had sustained the twins on a diet of cornflower, arrowroot, wine and water; no wonder they had not survived. In her frustration, she was heard to shout and swear at the children. 'I wish both the...children were corpses! I wish that the b...things were in hell! I wish the whole lot were...corpses!' But did these angry words, uttered by countless frustrated and often desperate parents over generations, mean murder in mind?

The jury did not believe the poor woman to be a killer and without retiring to consider their verdict they acquitted Louisa Maniford. However, before she left the dock a free woman, the judge told Louisa to abstain in future from using language which 'every decent man, woman and child who heard it must have been shocked to listen to.' Mary Ann and Sarah Ann Maniford were interred in Yeovil Cemetery, without a ceremony of committal, on 19 January 1875 and lie side by side in unmarked common graves, B 1887 and 1888. Emma Pople lies not far away.

WHEN DEATH RODE
THE SKIMMINGTON

There was a form of rough justice exercised by our ancestors called Skimmerton Riding, Riding the Skimmington, Riding the Stang and many other local dialectic variations which stretch back into the mists of time.

In 1834 Roberts wrote in his *History of Lyme Regis* that the custom of 'skimmington riding still continues to hold its ground. Skimmington riding is a great moral agent, not perhaps so much in restraining the vicious as in causing them to shun public observation, thereby not holding out bad examples to the rising youth of both sexes; in a word, it checks those instances of openly profligate and licentious conduct, which else might become too prevalent among the lower orders, who cannot, like their superiors, have recourse to legal proceedings against the person who has injured them, or divorce; it brands with infamy all gross instances of licentiousness, and exposes to lasting ridicule those couples who by their dissensions disturb the quiet and order of the neighbourhood, and so set a bad example either by struggling for domestic ascendancy, or by their quarrelsome dispositions. A skimmington riding makes people laugh, but the parties for whom they ride never lose the ridicule and disgrace to which it attaches.'

The skimmington ride took many forms and in 1884 one is described as having taken place at Whitchurch Canonicorum in West Dorset, when the *Bridport News* reported that at about six o'clock in the evening of 5 November 'a strange noise was heard as of the sound of trays and kettles, and it was soon found that a "skimmerton-riding" was in progress, such a thing not having been known for years in this parish. Three grotesquely attired figures were seen to be escorted by a procession consisting of persons dressed in various queer and eccentric costumes and who paraded the parish ... The figures alluded to appeared to the villagers to represent three personages who were well known to them, there being a male and two females, whose past conduct had caused them to be made the subject of this queer exhibition ... One of the females was represented as having an extraordinary long tongue which was tied back to the neck, whilst in one hand she held some note paper, and in the other a pen and holder. Those forming the procession were literally 'wetted' at the various inns, and after their perambulations were concluded they repaired to a certain field where a gallows was erected, and on which the effigies were hung and afterwards burnt ... The extraordinary proceedings were terminated with a fight, in which black eyes and bloody noses were not absent.'

On the north wall of the Great Hall of Montacute House there are two early seventeenth century plasterwork panels which depict a hen-pecked husband having a quick drink of ale whilst he baby-sits. He is set upon by his wife and a neighbour who witnesses the scene tells the village. The husband is then depicted 'riding the skimming-ton' sitting on a pole and being paraded around the village to the jeers of his neighbours.

Riding the skimmington could be physically cruel as shown in a case in Yeovil in 1845. On this occasion a gang of builders who suspected that one of their number had been stealing their dinners, sat him on a rafter and paraded him through the streets with the words 'A Thif' written on a board tied to his back. One of the local newspapers reported that the 'lynchers who had recreated this almost obsolete punishment of 'riding the stang' had contrived to refine the cruelty of the punishment by sharpening to a point the rafter on which the unfortunate fellow rode and by jagging him at several places. He was taken home to Bradford Abbas in a cart being so much injured as to be unable to walk.' The incident so outraged local opinion that nine of the workmen were prosecuted and received short terms of imprisonment for riot and assault.

The skimmington sometimes took the form of men and youths parading in front of an 'offender's' house and making 'rough music' by beating kettles, trays, buckets and anything else which would make a loud noise. Although generally harmless, the resulting stigma could lead to a family or individual moving away and on at least one occasion, riding the skimmington proved fatal.

The quiet of the spring evening was shattered by the beating of kettles, old tin trays, cans and other assorted hardware and the shouts of a score of young men as they started up a 'rough band outside old Kitty Shears' cottage in Shepton Montague. Backwards and forwards they marched shouting that the skimmington was riding for Betty Beach who, with her labourer husband John and her four children, lived with the old lady. Betty Beach had committed the ultimate 'sin' of usurping the male role when she stopped two boys from fighting and had given one of them a good hiding; in Shepton

Montague, and no doubt in many other villages, women did not 'wear the breeches' and give boys, other than their sons, a beating. The skimmington was riding to put the matter right and Betty Beach in her place.

The door of the cottage flew open and in the gathering dusk, the frail figure of old Kitty Shears could be seen silhouetted in the lamp light of the parlour.

'Be off, go away, be off, what do'ee want making thik noise!' screeched the old lady to the cheers and louder beating of the rough band which proceeded unabated. In her anger and frustration, Kitty Shears shuffled to the wall of her front garden and picking out some loose stones, threw them at the jeering mob.

Suddenly the old lady squealed and fell forward against the wall where she began to groan pitifully before she turned and staggered back into her cottage and the door was slammed behind her. The 'band' fell silent, and when someone shouted, 'She be bad hurt!', it melted away.

Katherine, to give Kitty her true forename, Shears, widow, aged seventy-six years, was hurt and fatally so, for early the next morning, 15 April 1871, she died. The local police made immediate enquiries and a neighbour, twenty-four-year-old Henry Trim, was taken into custody on suspicion of throwing a stone at Kitty Shears and killing her.

On 19 April, the coroner, Dr Wybrants, held an inquest on the body of the old lady and the first witness to be called was Edwin Brown, an apprentice harness-maker from nearby Bruton. He told the jury that on the evening of Friday 14 April between eight and nine o'clock, he had been a spectator of the skimmington outside Kitty Shears' cottage and had watched the young men and boys beating the rough music. Brown had seen the old lady come out of the cottage and shout at the crowd to go away but when this had no effect he saw her throw some stones at the 'band' which was standing some 30 feet away on the opposite side of the road. The witness then told how he had seen Henry Trim put down the kettle he had been beating, pick up a large stone and throw it at Kitty Shears with such force that he had heard a loud thud when it hit her chest. He saw no other stones thrown at the old lady.

Edwin Brown stated that when the crowd broke up, Henry Trim, knowing that the witness had seen him throw the stone, suggested that he had been mistaken and that someone else was the culprit. The next witness, John Hobbs, corroborated Edwin Brown's testimony. Dr Edmund Heginbothom, of Bruton, told the jury that he had carried out the post mortem examination of the deceased and stated that, in his opinion, the injury caused by the stone was sufficient to cause death.

The jury returned a verdict of manslaughter against Henry Trim and he was committed to Shepton Mallet Gaol to await trial at the Wells Summer Assizes.

On Friday, 3 August 1871, Henry Trim appeared before Mr Justice Willes charged with the manslaughter of Katherine Shears at Shepton Montague. When asked how he pleaded, Trim replied that he did not know whether he was guilty or not, because others were throwing stones and he never saw the old woman. Counsel for the prosecution was Mr Hooper but before he could open the case, the judge was told that the prisoner's solicitor had not given his brief to Mr Saunders, the counsel employed for the defence. However Mr Justice Willes saw no reason for delay and instructed the case to proceed.

The prosecution outlined the events of the evening of 14 April which had led to the death of Katherine Shears and Mr Hooper called Edwin Brown who recounted his evidence given at the inquest. However, under cross examination by Mr Saunders, Brown retracted the part of his evidence in which he stated that he had seen the prisoner deliberately throw the stone at Kitty Shears. The witness now stated that he had not seen the stone strike the old lady and Henry Trim had thrown the stone with no particular aim. When asked by the Judge whether this statement appeared on the depositions, Mr Hooper confirmed that it did not, and Mr Justice Willes suggested that in the light of these new circumstances the prosecution might consider whether to continue with the case as the death would seem to be accidental. Following the Judge's remarks Mr Hooper stated that the prosecution would not press the case any further.

Mr Justice Willes then turned to the jury and said that without doubt this was a deplorable accident, stones had been thrown but the witness Brown had testified that the stone which had caused the death of the old woman had been thrown without aim or malice. Although the jury could continue with the case, the judge believed that after the admission of the witness Brown, it would be useless to endeavour to convict on the evidence now before them. The prisoner had been in gaol for three months and he considered this to have been sufficient punishment for accidentally causing the death of Katherine Shears

After a short consultation, the jury found the prisoner not guilty, and following a caution from Mr Justice Willes against throwing stones in future, a very relieved, and perhaps wiser, Henry Trim went home to his wife, Martha, and young son waiting in Shepton Montague.

But why did Edwin Brown change his evidence and where was John Hobbs who had corroborated it at the inquest? Did they fear that the skimmington might ride for them?

THE FIGHT AT THE RUNNING HORSE

Henry Phillips kicked over the stool and presenting his not too steady fists to the soldier of the 67th Regiment of Foot, challenged him to a fight. Too much ale and cider had been downed at the Running Horse beer house in the aptly named Wine Street in Yeovil during that Saturday afternoon on 25 March 1843 and some of the drinkers were in a fighting mood.

The soldier stripped off his tunic but, before the two men could set about each other, big William Crocker stepped between them. Crocker was a strong and hard fighting man, and liked everyone to know it.

'There'll be no fighting while I be here!' Crocker announced pushing Phillips away from the soldier. 'I be the best fighting man in this town and no one can say any different.'

'Is that a fact, then perhaps I'll have to prove that I be a better man than thee!' came the challenge from Rifleman George Watkins of the Rifle Brigade who, like the soldier of the 67th Foot, was recruiting in the town, and lodging at the Running Horse.

'Done!' responded Crocker, and stripping off their jackets, the two men went out into the beer house yard followed by fellow drinkers and Crocker's wife.

Later, one of the spectators, Robert Anning, a local butcher, would recall the events which followed and how he had watched Crocker and the soldier square up to fight. Both men traded blows but Crocker soon broke through his opponent's guard and with a massive punch sent him crashing against the wall of the yard. As he fell Watkins' head struck a protruding stone and he slid to the ground, dazed. Crocker bent down and, grabbing the front of the soldier's shirt, pulled him to a sitting position and back-handed him hard across the face. Despite the blows, Watkins staggered to his feet, only to be battered to the ground and then hit about the head by Crocker's wife.

This was too much for some of the spectators, who shouted 'Unfair, unfair', and Crocker stood back. Despite the beating, Watkins was still game to continue and seconds were appointed, a man called Grey for the soldier, and Henry Leach for Crocker. The fight resumed, but within a short time Watkins was bleeding profusely from his nose and mouth and from cuts around his eyes; he was spared further punishment by the arrival of the town police who stopped the unequal contest.

Alfred Etheredge, one day to become Yeovil's first full-time town surveyor, was busy in his father's accounts office in Wine Street when he heard the commotion in the yard of the Running Horse. Going out to investigate, he found the gate to the yard bolted, but, peering through a crack, he could see the fight. After watching for a few minutes he hurried back to his cash books and finished the balancing but, hearing the continuing row from the beer house, he returned to his spy hole. The fighting had finished but some people were still milling about in the yard and Alfred caught a glimpse of one the men, whom he identified later as George Watkins, being helped back indoors.

Coach builder John A'Court was working in Mr King's carriage works next door to the Running Horse and when the row started up he looked over the wall to see what was going on. He would later describe the unequal contest and how the soldier had been badly beaten.

George Watkins was taken into the kitchen of the beer house where, for a while, Crocker continued to shower abuse on the battered rifleman who was too bemused to respond. He was given some cider which made him very sick and, because of his condition, the soldier was put to bed.

A local surgeon, Mr Arnold Coles, was walking along Wine Street on the following Wednesday when Rifleman Watkins came out of the Running Horse and asked for his advice. The soldier told the surgeon that he had been feeling very unwell for the past few days and was suffering from a severe headache which would not go away. Observing the bruising about the man's eyes and forehead, Mr Coles enquired how this had occurred. Watkins explained that he had been walking along by the River Yeo and had slipped down the bank hitting his head as he fell into the cold water. Because he was shivering and appeared feverish, the surgeon took the soldier back into the beer house where, after bleeding him, sent him to bed with some medicine.

Mr Coles was pleased to note some improvement when he visited his patient the next day but Watkins' condition began to deteriorate during the following week. It was now that the soldier's landlady told the surgeon about the fight and, asked why he had not told the truth, George Watkins said that he thought Mr Coles would consider it to be disgraceful behaviour.

The soldier's condition worsened daily but, despite constant medical attention, he died at four o'clock in the morning of 12 April 1843.

Mr Coles and a colleague surgeon, Mr William Shorland, carried out the postmortem, and finding great congestion of the brain and its blood vessels, concluded that this had been caused by blows to the head, aggravated by exposure to cold, and that death had resulted.

The inquest was held by the coroner, Mr Caines, in the Moon Inn, on Good Friday 15 April. The jury proceeded to view the body of George Watkins which was lying in the Running Horse and it was reported that the deceased was 'a very fine-grown good-looking man' but who presented a 'sad spectacle from the injuries received in a fight.'

Robert Anning, Alfred Etheredge and John A'Court, came forward as witnesses and testified how unfair the fight had been. Following the evidence of Mr Coles that death had resulted from the blows to the head, the jury returned a verdict of 'Manslaughter against William Crocker by fighting the said George Watkins on the 25th March and that he died in consequence thereof on the 12th April, instant.' The coroner issued a warrant for the arrest of Crocker who had fled the town following the soldier's death, and he was subsequently arrested in Crewkerne a few days later.

Crocker was brought before Mr Justice Coleridge at the Somerset Lammas Assizes in Bridgwater at nine o'clock on the morning of Saturday, 12 August 1843 and indicted for feloniously killing George Watkins by striking and beating and throwing him to the ground. A second charge was added indicting Crocker for common assault. Prosecuting counsel was Mr Fitzherbert and Mr Kinglake defended the prisoner.

Mr Fitzherbert opened by recounting the events of 25 March and concluded by declaring that Watkins had died following the ferocious conduct of the prisoner. He called Alfred Etheredge and John A'Court who repeated their evidence given at the inquest. The third witness, Robert Anning, told how he had watched the fight from start to finish and added that both men had been drinking heavily before they fought. He stated that at one stage the soldier of the 67th Foot had punched the deceased.

Mr Coles, the surgeon, explained the treatment he had applied to Watkins before he died and gave details of the postmortem examination. He confirmed his opinion, given at the inquest, that death was the result of 'affection of the head caused by blows.' Counsel for the prisoner asked whether the ducking in the River Yeo could have contributed to the 'affection of the head' and Mr Coles agreed that being immersed in very cold water could cause similar appearances in the brain.

Re-examined by the prosecution Mr Coles stated that he had observed the marks of blows about the deceased's eyes and face but none on the head. In reply to a question by Mr Justice Coleridge, the surgeon confirmed that the injuries to the face and the appearance of the brain were what he would expect to see after a hard fight with blows struck and death following.

Mr Kinglake then rose and addressed the jury. He stated that without doubt this was a very serious case and one which required calm consideration. No man should consider the case without a proper feeling of regret at the unfortunate end of the life of the deceased. Mr Kinglake certainly hoped that no one who had heard the case would feel it so deeply as the prisoner at the bar. However, the jury should not come to the conclusion that the prisoner had been the cause of Watkins' death unless the evidence perfectly satisfied them that he had. Counsel thought that the statement of his learned friend that the prisoner was guilty of ferocious conduct had not been exactly proved, but, on the contrary, if it had not been for the challenge of the deceased, there would have been no fight. The prisoner at the bar was a peaceable man, he had prevented one fight, and it was only because he had said that he was the best man in the town and would allow no fighting that he had received the challenge. The following fight was one of those common public house quarrels which ought always to be avoided, but which everyone knew took place all too frequently. Blows were struck on both sides and both men had knocked each other down. The deceased had received blows about the eyes and forehead which had caused some bleeding, but this was nothing extraordinary! Was there any evidence that one single blow had been the cause of death? There was not! The deceased had also been struck by the prisoner's wife and the soldier of the 67th Foot, and in no way could the prisoner be answerable for these blows.

And, what had the surgeon told them? He had examined the brain and found inflammation which he had stated was the cause of death. The surgeon had agreed, however, that no matter how the inflammation had been brought about, it would have caused death. Therefore if the deceased had fallen into the river and got wet and very cold, this could also have accounted for the inflammation.

Mr Kinglake announced that he would prove that only a few days before the fight the deceased had fallen into the River Yeo and afterwards appeared to be very ill. Because the surgeon had testified that cold could have been a cause of death, he believed the jury would conclude that the demise of Watkins had not arisen from the violence committed by the prisoner in the fight.

Counsel then called William Dawe of Misterton who recounted that, on the Thursday before 25 March, he had been walking with George Watkins along the bank of the River Yeo near Compton Mill and they had been looking for a place to jump across. They finally found one but when the soldier jumped he had landed heavily and rolled down the bank into the river. Watkins had remained in the freezing water for some time trying to get out but, when he had finally succeeded, the solder was exhausted, shivering and appeared to be very ill.

In summing up, Mr Justice Coleridge stated that if in a fair fight one man struck another and killed him he would be guilty of manslaughter. The jury had heard from the surgeon that the cause of death was somewhat in doubt and could have been caused by external violence, or by cold from being in the water. If there was any doubt as to which of these was the cause of death, then the prisoner was entitled to a verdict of not guilty. However, if the jury acquitted him of the crime of manslaugher, the judge suggested that they could not acquit the prisoner of the assault. It was an assault for one man to strike another.

After some considerable discussion, the jury found William Crocker not guilty of the manslaughter of George Watkins but guilty of an assault.

The judge addressed the prisoner and told him that the verdict was a proper one. Although the learned counsel for the defence had lightly described the occurrence at the beer house as no more than a drunken squabble, he did not consider that this was a very favourable description of this violent act. Sadly this was only one out of a thousand instances of the results of quarrels 'occasioned by the love which the common people of this country have for intoxicating liquor.'

Mr Justice Coleridge then sentenced William Crocker to six months penal servitude.

It was, no doubt, a very relieved William Crocker who later that day set out on the short journey to the County Gaol in Taunton rather than the much longer one which would have been his lot if he had been found guilty of manslaughter and sentenced to be transported to Australia for life.

THE EXTRAORDINARY
CASE OF INFANTICIDE
AT CREWKERNE

*It began as a quarrel between two serving girls
and ended with a man on trial for his life.*

The town of Crewkerne was full of gossip and excited speculation in the early summer of 1843. A wealthy man, the son of a
banker, was being questioned about the death of an illegitimate
child born to his young female servant. This was the stuff of novel-
ettes and the *Taunton Courier* exclaimed that if the statements 'are to
be believed, the circumstances have, fortunately, no parallel in our
criminal annals.'

Martha Clarke, servant of Mr Richard Alven, a yeoman farmer
worth a considerable fortune living in Sheep Market Street, had
rowed with Sarah Bulgin about a suggested pregnancy. Sarah, who
had been a servant some years before in the Alven household, had
been spreading gossip and had accused Martha Clarke of concealing
the birth of her illegitimate child. Although Martha had strenuously
denied the accusation and had challenged Sarah Bulgin to hold her
tongue, the rumours soon reached the ears of the parish authorities
and questions were being asked.

Matters came to a head on 19 May when Martha was charged by
John Turner, one of the town policemen, with having disposed of her
illegitimate child. Protesting her innocence, the girl was lodged in
custody at Turner's house, but just after breakfast the following day
Martha broke down and began to cry bitterly. The policeman's wife,
Elizabeth, tried to comfort the weeping girl who suddenly blurted
out, 'If I'm had up before the magistrate today I'll confess all about it!'

'What do you mean Martha?' enquired the older woman.

'I've had a child but I don't know nothing more about it and if I
suffer, that Alven shall also!' Martha cried, and then out poured the
story. The girl confessed that she had been put in the family way by
her master, Richard Alven, and in the afternoon of the Sunday before
last Christmas Day, she had given birth to the baby in the hay loft of
the house in Sheep Market Street. Martha went on to tell how Alven
had delivered the baby and had then taken it away. Although she

had never seen it, she was convinced that the child had been born alive because she had heard it cry. The girl then recounted that she had gone back into the house and pretended that she had never been confined. Martha related bitterly how afterwards her master had done nothing for her, and concluded by saying that when Alven's dog had had pups, he had made gruel for it and she told him that he had behaved kinder to his dog than to her.

And there it was, the rumours made fact, and when John Turner returned home from his morning's duties, the story was retold to him.

Martha was taken before the town magistrates and a warrant was issued for Richard Alven's house to be searched for the missing child. John Turner was despatched with the warrant but although he combed the garden, hay loft and stable, he found no trace of an infant, dead or alive. However, the damning statement had been made and Richard Alven was taken into custody for questioning.

By now the whole neighbourhood was in a state of exquisite excitement made more dramatic by the characters involved.

Richard Alven was 30 years of age and a bachelor. He was rich and said to be worth £18,000 and was also eccentric and a bit of a recluse, living with only his cousin Miss Charlotte Coles, to keep house and one servant, Martha Clarke. Martha was about twenty, although she said later that she did not know when she was born, and was described as a 'rather good looking country girl.' Here, therefore, were all the ingredients of a Victorian melodrama about to be acted out in the small town of Crewkerne where there had been little excitement since the Civil War of two centuries before.

Both Richard Alven and Martha Clarke were taken to the County Gaol at Taunton and the questioning continued during the next few weeks, Alven protesting his innocence but Martha continuing to point the accusing finger at him. However, there was no corpse and unless one could be found without much more delay, there would be no case.

On 10 June, following a visit by Mr Loveridge, one of the divisional magistrates, Martha Clarke made a statement indicating where she thought the child might have been buried. The following morning saw the constable of Crewkerne, Hugh Simmonds, and the two town policemen, John Turner and William Pottenger, make their way to the Alven house and begin to dig under bushes near the top of the enclosed garden. About a foot down they found the badly decomposed body of what appeared to be a small child. Surgeon, Mr Emmanuel Bowdage, was called and taking one of the spades and

Hugh Simmonds another, the two men lifted the small corpse out of the hole and onto a board. As they inspected the putrid mess, all four could see that a band of straw was wrapped around it. The corpse was taken to the Red Lion Inn and placed in a store room to await the arrival of the coroner.

Events were now moving fast. The inquest was held on Monday 12 June and the jury's verdict 'that the body now found is the body of a human being, an infant, but how or by whom placed there is not known', left the case open for further enquiry.

The magistrates opened their inquiry on Thursday 16 June in the Crewkerne Justice Room and Richard Alven and Martha Clarke were brought from the County Gaol through streets crammed with towns-people eager to catch a glimpse of the pair. Mr Langworthy of Ilminster prosecuted and Alven was represented by Mr Lowman and Mr Sparks; no one represented Martha Clarke.

Hugh Simmonds and William Pottenger testified to the finding of the body and Mr Emmanuel Bowdage gave the medical evidence. The surgeon recalled that at about a quarter before one on the previous Sunday he had been called to Richard Alven's garden and shown the corpse of an infant lying in a hole. He had assisted in the removal of the body and it had been taken to the Red Lion Inn where on the following morning he had examined it in the company of Mr Wills, a fellow surgeon. Mr Bowdage stated that the body was of a 'full grown infant much decomposed' and twisted around it was a band of hay and straw. There were traces of blood on the band which the surgeon believed came from the child and suggested that it had been born alive; if the child had been still-born he considered that there would have been no blood. Decomposition was too far advanced for the sex of the infant to be established.

Sarah Bulgin was called and said that she had been a servant of Mr Alven until Martha Clarke took her place about two years ago. She had noticed how big Martha was becoming and when they were gleaning corn together at the last harvest she had joked about her being in the family way. As the weeks passed, the girl seemed to be getting bigger and bigger, but then one day Sarah had visited Mr Alven's house and Martha Clarke was smaller and looked ill. When she had said, 'Why Martha you have lost your belly', there had been no reply. Sarah Bulgin admitted that she was unmarried and had two young children.

The next two witnesses, Mrs Mary Fowler and Miss Charlotte Coles, were called to confirm Martha Clarke's statement about some of the events on the afternoon of Sunday 18 December.

Mary Fowler said that she had been a servant to Mr Alven's late father and now was married to a local farmer. She knew Martha Clarke but on the few occasions she had seen her recently had observed no signs of pregnancy. However, in the morning of the Sunday in question, Miss Coles had called on her and said that she was troubled about some stories that Martha Clarke was in the family way. Although Martha had strenuously denied the rumours, Miss Coles wished to put her mind at rest and asked Mary Fowler to come to the house later that afternoon and have a look at the girl.

Mary Fowler recounted that at about four o'clock she called at the Alven house and whilst she was talking to Miss Coles in the hall, Richard Alven had come through from the rear passage. She was surprised when he did not greet her in his usual friendly manner and did not, as he always did on the previous occasions she called, invite the farmer's wife to see the household cows and the garden; he also seemed rather impatient with her being there. Shortly after, Mr Alven went back out again.

Mrs Fowler said that Miss Coles told her that Martha Clarke was out milking the cows and so the two women sat down and chatted. About an hour later she heard Martha come into the kitchen and begin pouring milk into a pail. Miss Coles then went out into the passage and, shortly after, Mary Fowler heard someone go upstairs.

When Miss Coles returned she said that Martha had not been feeling well and had gone up to her room. A few moments later someone called at the backdoor asking for Martha but when Miss Coles called up and told her, Mary Fowler heard the girl reply that if anyone wanted to see her they would have to go up as she still felt ill. It was then, Mary Fowler said, that Miss Coles asked her to go up and see what was wrong. The farmer's wife found Martha lying in bed complaining that she had been feeling poorly since last night. She said that she had been out the day before with the donkey cart and had run about and got very warm. Afterwards she had stood about and got cold. Suddenly Martha exclaimed, 'Mary! You know it had been reported a good deal about me that I be in the family way. Well I'm not! Here! feel me belly to prove it,' and grabbing her hand, the girl passed it over her stomach. Mary Fowler stated that Miss Coles had now arrived on the landing outside the room and called out to Martha that if she did not go downstairs at once, she would call the doctor to see her. The farmer's wife went out onto the landing and suggested to Miss Coles that they talk about the servant's condition before anything was done and both women went down to the parlour where they found Mr Alven sitting at the table.

Mary Fowler recalled that Richard Alven was wearing his old coat but could not remember whether his hands had been newly washed. Some cocoa was made and as the three sat drinking they discussed Martha Clarke. There was some concern at the rumours that she was in the family way but Mary Fowler stated that she told Mr Alven and Miss Coles that there were no signs of pregnancy. The possibility that the girl had been confined elsewhere in the town was discussed but this was dismissed as unlikely because the servant's duties required her to be about the house and garden all day.

Mary Fowler went on to say that when the conversation finished she took a cup of cocoa up to Martha and was followed by Miss Coles carrying a candle. Whilst the girl drank, Miss Coles had stood holding the candle at the half-opened door but when Mary Fowler came back onto the landing with the empty cup she enquired in a whisper whether anything was wrong. The farmer's wife said that as she could not be certain, Miss Coles had told her to go back again and this time to check the bed. In the flickering light of the candle, this time held at the fully-opened door, Mary Fowler examined the bed and the day clothes which Martha had been wearing. She found some marks of blood, but they were, in Mary's opinion, no more than could be expected from a young woman at certain times.

Returning down stairs, Mary Fowler told Miss Coles that the servant was not in the family way and then went home at about half past six. Mary Fowler told the court that she had spoken frankly about Martha's condition in the presence of Mr Alven because, when he was a young man, he had spent some time as a pupil of Mr Bowdage, the surgeon, and therefore she considered him to be like a doctor.

Now Charlotte Coles was called and stated that she lived with her cousin and managed his household. Martha Clarke had been in service for about two years and until the rumours began before Christmas last she had given no cause for complaint. The servant's duties included watering, feeding, milking and bedding down the household cows and, on occasion, she would be assisted by Mr Alven. Miss Coles went on to say that during early December it had been widely rumoured that Martha Clarke was with child but when asked whether these rumours were true the girl had strongly denied them. However, Miss Coles explained, she was not completely satisfied because she thought Martha was looking a little stout, but when she had told the girl to do up her coat she had been able to do so. To lay the rumours to rest, Miss Coles stated that she had decided to ask Mary Fowler, the former family servant and a respectable married woman with children, to have a look at Martha and find out whether she was in the family way

Miss Coles recalled that on the Sunday in question, Martha Clarke had partaken of her lunch as usual at one o'clock and then gone out into the back premises. She did not see her again until the milk was brought in later in the afternoon and she helped the girl to strain it into pails. She said that Martha had complained of feeling unwell, and as the milk was being taken down into the cellar she heard the girl go upstairs.

The witness then recounted the events described by Mary Fowler. With regard to her cousin's activities during the afternoon, Miss Coles remembered that he was in and about the house and garden and did not leave the premises. She could not recall whether he had helped with the cows or whether his behaviour to Mary Fowler was any different.

Edith Turner, the wife of the town policeman, was the next witness and told of Martha Clarke's confession at her house but denied that she had induced the girl to make the statement.

All the witnesses had now been called and Richard Alven was asked whether he wished to address the Court. 'Thank you gentlemen,' he replied, 'I am innocent of the charge.'

Martha Clarke, who was sitting opposite, leapt to her feet and pointing at Alven, shouted, 'He is not innocent, gentlemen!'

The *Taunton Courier*'s correspondent described the scene in suitably graphic detail. 'The sensation created by the exclamation was similar to the influence of an electric shock, excitement and agitation were visible in the countenances of everyone in the Court and it was some time before anything like quietness could be restored.'

When order was restored, the chairman told Martha that if she wished to address the court, now was the time to do so, but it was his duty to warn her that what she said would be taken down and if necessary used against her 'in another place.'

Martha Clarke was a lowly servant girl; she could not afford counsel, expensive or otherwise, to give her the benefit of legal advice or look after her interests and so she did what anyone in her lonely and desperate situation would have done. She told what she believed to have been the truth of what happened.

This is what she said in her own words:

I was delivered of a child and the prisoner Alven took it from me. He delivered me himself, it was on the Sunday before Christmas day last. He twisted a hayband and tied it round the child's neck and threw it amongst the reed. He never allowed me to see the child and he would never tell me whether it was a boy or a girl because if no one saw it I should never blush if accused by any one. As soon as I was delivered he told me to go down. I heard the child cry before and after I went down. I was in the hayloft about 10 minutes after the child was born and about 10 minutes after I was confined I went down and fetched the milking pail and brought it up to milk the cows. Alven carried the milk as far as the kitchen door and I took it up and carried it in and placed it on the table. I then went up stairs and went to bed. I asked Miss Coles for some more clothes which she denied me and she said I should have no more. Mary Fowler afterwards brought me some which Miss Coles gave her. I had been in bed about half an hour when Mary Fowler came up to me. She examined me and heaved up the bedclothes and did not think there was any more the matter with me than with any other woman. Miss Coles was standing outside my bedroom. I saw Alven place the hayband round something and heard it cry. It was moonlight at the time and there are windows in the place. When he was twisting the hayband his back was towards me, and after it was tied he threw it amongst the reed. I heard the child cry after I came down from the loft. I left him there and he returned about 5 minutes afterwards. I never heard the child cry after Alven came down. He never told me where the child was but I suspected it was somewhere in the garden. The day after I was confined I went into the garden and saw the ground had been removed at the top of the garden near the middle walk but I never examined the ground. I was in the stable at the time I was taken in labour, and Alven told me to go up into the hay loft and he said it was the best place. I never asked him what had become of the child. Mr Alven was the father of the child. He talked to me much about my being with child. He said he knew what was the matter with me but he never mentioned that he should deliver it himself. I had provided the clothes myself and gave it to my sister to keep until I wanted it. I purchased it myself. Mr Alven never suggested the getting of any clothes for the child. I never left his service. The gate of the garden door is secured so that no person could enter from the street. That is all I have to say.

The confession caused further uproar in the court and once again it took some time to quell. Following a short retirement, the magistrates committed both prisoners for trial at the next Assizes, Richard Alven as principal in the murder and Martha Clarke as accessory after the fact. An application for bail for Alven was refused, and both prisoners were 'ironed' and conveyed to the County Gaol.

Richard Alven appeared before Mr Justice Coleridge at the Somerset Lammas Assizes in Bridgwater on Wednesday 16 August 1843 indicted for 'the wilful murder of a child, name and sex unknown, on 18 December, 1842 in the Parish of Crewkerne, by tying a band of hay round its neck and thereby strangling it.' The prisoner, who was described as being respectably clad but with a forbidding countenance, in a clear voice pleaded 'Not Guilty!'

The charge of being an accessory after the fact against Martha Clarke had been dropped, and she would be presented as the prosecution's principal witness. Mr Kinglake and Mr Rawlinson appeared for the Crown and Mr Cockburn and Mr Stone defended.

The case for the prosecution opened by Mr Kinglake describing the events leading up to the fatal Sunday. He told the court that the prisoner had resided in Crewkerne for some years and was a man of considerable property. The charge against him was that in the latter part of 1842 the female servant, who lived with the prisoner and his cousin, Miss Coles, was in the family way by him, and, that in December a child was born alive and he had killed it. The servant, Martha Clarke, would state that she was in the family way, the prisoner was the father and that on the afternoon of the Sunday before Christmas in 1842, the pain of labour came upon her and she was delivered of a child. The witness would state that the prisoner knew she was in the family way, that he had spoken frequently to her on the subject, and would give details of his actions on the afternoon in question. Mr Kinglake concluded by emphasising that the substance of the indictment depended upon the credit which the jury would place on the statement of Martha Clarke. The defence would almost certainly seek to discredit her evidence as she had been an accomplice and party to the crime but, after hearing what she had to say, he would submit that she was not an accomplice.

The constable of Crewkerne and William Pottenger were then called and gave evidence of the finding of the corpse.

Mr Bowdage, the surgeon, recounted the evidence of the removal of the body from the garden and his subsequent examination. Cross-examined by Mr Cockburn he stated that he had not put the bones together or measured the child because it was too badly decomposed and in his opinion it had been in the ground for some five to six months. The state of decomposition was such that he could not confirm that it had been born alive. However, the blood found on the hayband could have flowed from the umbilical cord if the child was born alive and it could also be fatal if the cord was not tied. Mr Bowdage stated that he did not think it likely that a woman just delivered of a child could carry a pail of milk or that she could get up the next morning. In reply to a question from the judge, the surgeon agreed that 'women of the lower orders go to work sooner after delivery than those in the better classes of life.'

The principal witness, Martha Clarke, now took the stand and it is not difficult to imagine how she must have felt as she entered the witness box under the gaze of judge, jury, lawyers and the mass of spectators thronging the court room.

In a clear voice Martha proceeded to tell how she had lived with Mr Alven as his servant and had found herself to be in the family way some twelve months after she had entered the household. Mr Alven was the father and she had spoken about her condition to him on a number of occasions and he had also observed it himself. At about 3 or four o'clock on the Sunday afternoon before Christmas she had been in the hall of the house when she had felt the pains coming on, and as she went out of the back door Alven had followed her and told her that the best place to go was to the hay loft. Martha stated that she followed his instruction and he went down to the cow house. She could not remember how long she lay in the loft but Alven kept visiting her to see how she was. Near the time of her confinement she had felt very ill and Alven had remained with her and then delivered the child. He then took the infant from her and she saw him twist a hayband. However, Martha then said that she did not see what became of the child neither did she know what Alven did with it or the hayband. He had said nothing about the child and he had not allowed her to see it. Alven had then told her to go down to the stable and wait and he would milk the cow. As she she was about to leave the loft, Martha was certain that she heard the child cry, and as she reached the bottom of the ladder she heard it cry again. Alven then came down, milked the cow in the stable and carried the milk to the back kitchen and Martha carried it from there into the house. When she got in she had gone up to her room and into bed. About ten minutes later Mary Fowler and Miss Coles came to the door of her room. Martha stated that she had stayed in bed all evening and all night, but got up again the next day and did a little work. She also noticed on the following day that the ground had been freshly turned near the top of the garden near the middle walk. Martha concluded by saying that Alven had told her at about eight o'clock of the Sunday morning that Miss Coles had been after Mary Fowler to look at her to see if she was in the family way.

Mr Cockburn, leading for the defence, now subjected Martha Clarke to a savage cross-examination but she did not waver from her story and although she became confused about the events in the hayloft, she maintained that Richard Alven was the father and that he had delivered the child.

The remaining witnesses, Sarah Bulgin, Mary Fowler and Charlotte Coles, repeated the evidence they had given before the magistrates. Elizabeth Turner told of Martha's first statement and firmly denied inducing or in any way encouraging the girl to confess.

Now came the time for Mr Cockburn to address the jury and he went into the attack. The prisoner, he said, stood accused on the testimony of one witness and he could not call evidence to prove that he was not a party to the 'transaction' with which he had been charged. His learned friend had pointed to the case depending entirely on the testimony of the principal witness and if the jury did not believe her then that was the end because there was nothing in the rest of the evidence to fix guilt upon this 'unhappy man.' It was said that Martha Clarke was not an accomplice. What then was she? She, by her own confession, had given birth to a child and being charged with having made away with it, she turned round and blamed in on her master, the prisoner at the bar!

Mr Cockburn then took each statement made by Martha Clarke and argued their improbability. He constantly pointed out to the jury that there was no evidence as to the mode of death and argued on the improbability of the mother of her first-born child acquiescing in the contemplated murder of her infant in the hay loft, without remonstrating against the deed. Could a master have had so much influence over his servant to suppress a mother's feelings for her child and become a party to its death? The prisoner had no motive to kill the child, he was not poor and the expense of maintaining it would have been of no consequence. It might be said that his character was at stake but he had no ground for fear of moral censure for he was not married and there was no reason why he should place himself in such dire peril of his life.

Mr Cockburn suggested to the jury that there were three things on which they must be satisfied. First, that the child had been born alive; second, that the prisoner had killed it and third, that it was killed in the manner described in the indictment.

KILLED FOR A PIECE OF BACON
*'Blood was on the grass banks and the hedges ...' Trendle Well Lane,
photographed in 1989, remained much the same as when Ruth Butcher
met her death in 1874*

'OTHING HAS EVER BEEN ADMINISTERED TO HER IN HER FOOD'
*The Boro', Yeovil, circa 1860. Silvester Peter's linen draper's shop with
its overhanging balcony is on the extreme left of the photograph*

THE DEVIL OF DEAD MAN'S POST
John Ball was hurrying over Staple Hill when he witnessed the fatal beating of young John Lane

THE UNTIMELY END OF CONSTABLE PENNY
The headstone in West Coker churchyard erected by the villagers as a testimony of their affection and respect for Constable Penny

THE KILLING OF DANDY JOE
After falling out over a game of skittles, Dandy Joe and Farmer Hodges
fought in the road on the right of the White Post Inn

WHO KILLED MR STUCKEY?
The high banks of the quiet road from Dinnington to Windwhistle provided an
ideal setting for the ambush of Mr Stuckey

'HOW YOUR HAND DO SHAKE, GEORGE'
George White killed his wife on this stretch of the road between
Inwood Lodge and Henstridge on a dark night in March 1883

'YE THOUGHTLESS YOUTHS A WARNING TAKE'
Edmund Horner's tombstone in Hinton St George churchyard
warns young men of the dangers of breaking the sabbath day

'WHAT A FOOL I'VE BEEN – I'VE NOT DONE IT YET'
Albion Wadman led Sergeant Smith and Constable Scadding from the Wincanton police station up Conygar Lane to where he had murdered his son

THE KILLING IN THE CLOVER FIELD
Kingsbury Bridge at Milborne Port crosses the stream into which James Osmond threw the blade of his scythe

THE SLAYING ON SANDPIT HILL

Sandpit Hill, on the road between Curry Rivel and Langport, near the spot where master plumber, John Harvey, was robbed and murdered by his apprentices

SUFFER THE LITTLE CHILDREN

Photographed in 1956, Park Street, Yeovil is little changed from the day in September 1874 when baby Emma Pople died in suspicious circumstance

WHEN DEATH RODE THE SKIMMINGTON
A serenade of 'rough music'

THE FIGHT AT THE RUNNING HORSE
High Street, Yeovil at the time of the fatal fight in the Running Horse Beerhouse

THE EXTRAORDINARY CASE OF INFANTICIDE AT CREWKERNE
*The tragic events of December 1842 took place in Market Street, Crewkerne
in the large house shown in the centre of the photograph*

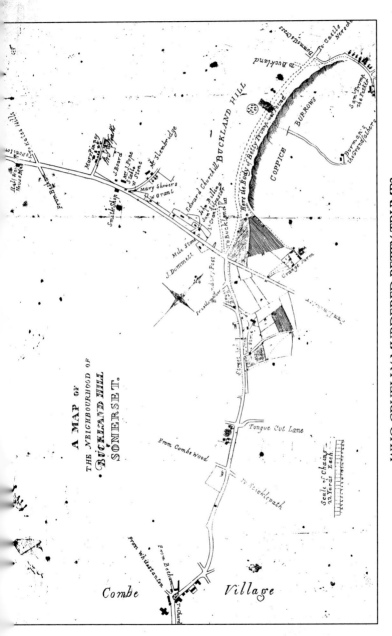

WHO CRUELLY MURDERED BETTY TRUMP?

The map annexed to the booklet published by William Flood shows the place where Betty Trump's body was found. Many of the houses shown on the map still remain adjoining the main A303 road

MURDER!

WHEREAS AN ATROCIOUS

Rape and Murder

Was committed on the NIGHT of MONDAY, the 30th. of November last, near the Town of CHARD, Somerset, on the Body of JOAN TURNER.

One Hundred Pounds
REWARD

Is hereby offered, to any Person (except the actual Perpetrator) who shall discover the *Offender or Offenders*, so as that *he* or *they* may be apprehended and convicted of the said MURDER; such *Reward* to be paid on conviction, on application to the *Portreve of the Borough of Chard*.

(Signed) W. LEMAN, *Portreve.*

TAKE NOTICE,

That all Persons having any information to give respecting the said MURDER, are requested to communicate it without delay, to Mr. SAMUEL EDWARDS, in CHARD aforesaid, the Secretary to the Committee, appointed to sit daily for investigating the same.

Chard, December 4th. 1829.

By order of the Committee,--SAMUEL EDWARDS, Secretary.

J. TOMS, PRINTER, BOOKBINDER, BOOKSELLER, STATIONER, &c. CHARD AND AXMINSTER.

'I AM FREE AND INNOCENT OF THE CRIME'
*The poster offering the substantial reward of £100
for the arrest of Joan Turner's killer*

'THAT FISHER'S MAD!'
This silhouette sketch of Joel Fisher was first published in the Westonian, *July 1844*

THE WITHYPOOL POISONER
A dish of cream liberally laced with arsenic brought sudden death to the remote Exmoor village of Withypool in the summer of 1829

THE MALIGNANT SHOOTING OF JOSEPH DUNFORD
The corpse of Joseph Dunford was taken to his cottage to await the surgeon's examination following the fatal shooting.
The Keeper's Lodge, Brockley Park, 1825

A JEALOUSY AS CRUEL AS THE GRAVE
The crossroads at Ridgehill, near Winford. The body of Mark Cox was found lying in the road where the trees overhang in the centre of the photograph

MRS ADLAM KILLS HER HUSBAND

The High Street in Regency Bath at the time Mrs Mary Adlam slew her violent, drunken husband

'IT SHALL BE A LIFE FOR A LIFE BEFORE I SLEEP'

JACOB WILKINS GOES A-COURTING – FOR THE LAST TIME
As he waited in Ilchester Gaol for the hangman, James Reynolds finally confessed to the murder and robbery of Jacob Wilkins on Midford Hill

WHO CUT THE ROPE? – THE RADSTOCK PIT DISASTER
This 'monkey bag' and candle holder on display at Radstock, Midsomer Norton and District Museum belonged to Leonard Dowling, one of the miners killed at the Wells Way Pit

THE SHOOTING OF JOHN DYER AT THE BELL

Stall Street, Bath in the first decade of the nineteenth century illustrated in Rambles

On the first point, there was no evidence, except that of Martha Clarke, that the child had been born alive, indeed the surgeon could not be certain that life had existed at the time of birth. As to the second point, there was no evidence to connect the prisoner with the murder. With regard to the third point, the jury must be satisfied that the death was occasioned in the manner described in the indictment, namely, that the prisoner had killed the child by tying a hayband around its neck and strangled and suffocated it. The evidence from the surgeon and the men who had discovered the body was that the hayband was tied round the body and there was nothing to show that it had caused strangulation.

The defending counsel went on to say that that there were several actions by the prisoner which proved his complete innocence. He had not sought to prevent Martha Fowler from examining Martha Clarke even though he knew his cousin would be asking her to do so. Neither had the prisoner, after the first examination of his house and garden by the town policeman, removed the corpse to a more secret place. Mr Cockburn concluded by suggesting to the jury that the case was surrounded by great doubt and suspicion and there was a total absence of all motive for the prisoner to commit the crime.

As he began his summing up, Mr Justice Coleridge turned to the jury and said that there was one important point which he wished to call to their attention, namely, that unless it was satisfactorily proved beyond all reasonable doubt that the death of the child had been caused in the manner described in the indictment, the prisoner could not be found guilty. He asked the jury to consider this point before he proceeded further, because if they were of the opinion that proof had not been given, it would be unnecessary for him to go through the whole of the evidence.

The jury consulted for a few minutes and decided that proof had not been given that the death had been caused by strangulation and found Richard Alven 'Not Guilty.'

Thus the melodrama was played out but not with the traditional ending, because in this production the 'Wicked Squire' had escaped his just deserts and the 'Tender Maiden' was made out to be a scheming liar.

And finally, was Richard Alven guilty? If not, did Martha Clarke give birth to another man's child, on her own, in the hay loft, and bury the body in the dark without anyone knowing it?

WHO CRUELLY MURDERED POOR BETTY TRUMP?

In the churchyard at Buckland St Mary, in the Blackdown Hills, there is a worn gravestone in memory of thirteen-year-old Betty Trump who was 'cruelly murdered' on the 20 February 1823. The village lies a little way off the London to Exeter road, and the pathetic body of poor Betty Trump was found in a thickly wooded area known as Coppice Burrows, a few hundred yards north of the present Eagle Tavern public house.

Betty, described as a 'fine smart girl, one of the prettiest in the neighbourhood,' was the daughter of Samuel Trump, a dairyman, who about a fortnight before the fatal day, had come from Winsham, near Chard to live in Buckland St Mary. However, Betty had been living in the village with her grandparents for a year before the Trump family arrived.

On Thursday 20 February, Mrs Elizabeth Trump asked Betty to go to Winsham to enquire whether she could live with Sarah, an older sister, who had stayed behind. She gave her daughter three shillings and sevenpence and told her to buy some plates, needles and thread and a pap spoon in Chard on the way back home.

Betty's walk to Winsham would take her along the Taunton to Chard turnpike road to the crossroads with the Ilminster to Honiton turnpike and then through Street Ash to Combe St Nicholas and Chard, a distance of about eight miles each way. The young girl was told to return home the same day, if possible.

The weather was fine when Betty left early on 20 February but Mrs Trump was not too worried when she did not come home that evening; perhaps it was asking a little too much to expect the thirteen-year-old to walk to Winsham and back before dark. However, when Betty had not arrived back before darkness fell the following evening, Samuel and Elizabeth became concerned, and first thing on the Saturday morning, daughter Ann was despatched to Winsham where she was alarmed to be told that Betty had left before three o'clock on Thursday afternoon.

On Ann's return late on Saturday afternoon, the worried parents began a search back along the road to Chard and before darkness called a halt, they established that Betty had bought the articles in the town and had been seen walking through Combe St Nicholas.

At first light next morning, Samuel Trump, his brother-in-law and a number of friends, began the search again and at about seven o'clock Daniel Parsons found the body in Coppice Burrows lying on its back about 50 yards from the Taunton to Chard turnpike road. Betty's throat had been cut but her clothing appeared to be intact and there were no signs of a struggle; her basket set down beside the body was undisturbed.

The grim news quickly spread through the neighbourhood and within a short time the wood was full of spectators who had hurried to the spot to 'view' the corpse. The coroner and parish officers were called and the body was removed to Samuel Trump's house at Dommett. Here the corpse was undressed and examined by Mr John Wheadon, a surgeon from Chard, who suggested that the girl's throat had been cut by a sharp instrument such as a knife or possibly a bill-hook, but he was somewhat vague about a possible sexual violation.

It was recorded that Betty Trump's burial was arranged for the following Sunday, but because over 1500 people came to view the body, the interment was deferred for another week during which time the coffin was repeatedly screwed down and re-opened for 'the gratification of the curious.' This was just one of a number of odd occurences arising from the tragic end of Betty Trump.

In the days which followed the discovery of the murder, the countryside was full of rumour and speculation. It was said that two strangers, dressed as sailors, had been seen in the vicinity of Buckland Hill and near Coppice Burrows at about the time the murder was thought to have been committed and Surgeon Wheadon suggested that the ferocity of the attack suggested more than one assailant. However, because of the time lapse between the murder and the discovery of the body, the strangers were long gone.

The inquest was held on Tuesday 25 February but the coroner was late and the jury, who had been summoned to attend at noon, did not begin their deliberations until seven o'clock that evening.

One of the witnesses to give evidence was William Flood, a twenty-six-year-old farm servant who lived with his master, Mr Samuel Wyatt of New House Farm, Buckland St Mary. Flood, who had known Betty Trump and taught her in the parish Sunday School, recalled hearing some cries for help and shouting coming from the direction of Coppice Burrows on the Thursday or Friday evening, he could not remember which, as he walked along the Ilminster to Honiton turnpike towards the small scatter of houses at Newtown. He said that he had taken little notice at the time because he thought a child was being beaten in one of the nearby cottages and when this happened it was not unusual for the victim to shout for help or cry murder.

When asked why he had not gone to find out what was causing the cries and why he had not mentioned this before, William Flood repeated that he did not consider it to have been his business and he had told Mr Wyatt about it after the murder had been discovered.

The coroner expressed some dissatisfaction with this reply and although the jury found that Betty Trump had been murdered by a person or persons unknown, the coroner's views were sufficient to fuel the rumour and gossip which had already started about William Flood. It was being said that he had arrived home late on the Thursday evening and refused to account for his absence, but more seriously that he had been 'in the habit of taking indecent liberties' with Betty Trump. In fact on the Sunday before her body was discovered, it was said that she had implored her mother not to let her go to Sunday School again. To add to the rumour mill there were stories of blood-stained clothes being found and burnt to remove the evidence which could convict William Flood.

The rumours and allegations were communicated to one of the local magistrates, the Reverend Dr Palmer, who issued a warrant for the arrest of William Flood on suspicion of the murder of Betty Trump. During the evening of 26 February, Joseph Salisbury, the constable, accompanied by Captains Bennet and Tucker, two local gentlemen, hastened to New House to secure the suspect. A search of Flood's room and examination of his clothes produced no incriminating evidence and a few spots of blood found on his working smock were proved to have been caused when he had helped Samuel Wyatt's nephew, John, kill a pig that morning. A blood-stained bill-hook was found but James Vickery, the Wyatt's farm boy, disclosed that he had used it recently to cut the horns off a dead sheep.

Nonetheless William Flood was taken into custody and on the next day was brought for examination before the Reverend Dr Palmer. The various allegations were heard by the magistrate who considered them to be unfounded and William Flood was released.

The decision was unacceptable to a number of the leading inhabitants of the area and a committee was formed to enquire into the murder. Although he had released William Flood, the Reverend Dr Palmer was anxious to solve the dreadful crime and administered an oath to the committee by which they bound themselves together to carry out the enquiries and not to disclose the information they obtained. One of the committee's first actions was to offer a reward of £100, equal to five years' wages for an agricultural labourer, and a considerable inducement to come forward with true evidence, or more sinisterly, with false. Approval was obtained from Sir Robert Peel, the Home Secretary, to offer a free pardon to anyone concerned with the murder, but who had not committed it, to turn King's Evidence.

The services of Mr Samuel Hercules Taunton, Bow Street runner, were obtained and on his arrival from London he began his investigations.

Several local men were questioned and released but William Flood continued to be the main suspect and on 8 March he was arrested by Mr Taunton and brought before the local magistrates who remanded him in custody in a small room at the Green Dragon Inn at Combe St Nicholas.

Two days after his arrest William Flood was questioned alone by Mr Samuel Taunton and asked to account for his movements on the day of the murder. He explained that he had been dung-spreading at Street Ash Farm and not hedge-laying or trimming with a billhook as rumoured in some quarters. Flood recalled seeing Betty Trump go by the field in which he was working early on the Thursday morning but he had not seen her again that day. Between a quarter and half past five he had stopped spreading and then fed the cattle in the yard at Street Ash Farm. With his work finished for the day he had walked home to New House Farm along the Ilminster to Honiton turnpike. On the way Flood recalled that he had met Miss Honor Marsh near the Bound Stone, a little way west of the crossroad, and shortly after he heard cries coming from the direction of some cottages towards Buckland Hill. He arrived at New House Farm at about a quarter-past six and his master and other people would swear to this.

The Bow Street runner had searched Flood's bedroom on the day he was arrested and found a small knife on the top of his box of possessions and the prisoner had handed over the knife he carried when at work. He had taken away the shirt Flood was wearing on the day of the murder but found no blood stains on it.

During the following weeks, the committee and the Bow Street runner continued to question the prisoner, interviewed over 40 prospective witnesses and engaged in a number of curious, if not highly irregular, activities. Although William Flood had been able to engage the services of an attorney, Mr Cox of Honiton, the lawyer was to encounter considerable obstruction from committee and the magistrates in obtaining access to his client and was not allowed to meet him until the first public hearing on 28 March.

On Good Friday, Phillip Wyatt, an unusual character known as the 'Carpenter, Poet and Soothsayer of the Western Parts of Somerset', was taken to the prisoner's room accompanied by Captain Bennet, one of the committee, and a strange conversation took place. The soothsayer told William Flood that he had lain three nights on Betty Trump's grave and on the third night her spirit appeared and had walked with him to the spot where the body had been found, conversing with him all the way respecting the murder. The spirit had accused William Flood of committing the murder and, after hovering over the spot where the body had lain, the spirit had vanished. Phillip Wyatt then took the prisoner's hand and holding it aloft had declared that 'this is the hand of a murderer, as Nathan said unto David, so I say unto thee, thou art the man!' The Soothsayer and Captain Bennet then left the room.

Another unusual method of seeking to establish William Flood's guilt was being widely practised during the weeks he lay incarcerated in the Green Dragon. A bible was opened and the front door key of the inquirer's house was placed upon the sixteenth verse of the first chapter of the Book of Ruth which reads, 'And Ruth said entreat me not to leave thee or to return from following after thee: for whither thou goest, I will go and where thou lodgest I will lodge: thy people shall be my people and thy God, my God.' The bible was closed and tightly bound, with the bow of the key left protruding. Two people would then hold the key between their forefingers and chant 'Did William Flood commit the murder?' followed by the verse. If the bible turned fully around before the verse was repeated, William Flood was judged guilty; if not , he was innocent. It was said that members of the committee indulged in this practice and the bible of the landlord of the Green Dragon was worn out at verse 16!

On another occasion Sir William Templer Pole, one of the committee members, visited the prisoner and told him that the evidence against him had been laid before the judges at the Exeter Assizes who were of the opinion that not only was there sufficient evidence to commit him to prison but to bring him to execution. Sir William went on to say that he expected the prisoner to be tried at the Taunton Assizes which were about to begin and he should prepare himself for death because he could not live beyond the coming Friday as only two days were allowed a guilty murderer after his trial.

Despite these highly irregular and almost certainly illegal activities, the committee were making progress and had established the probable timetable leading up to the murder of Betty Trump on 20 February.

Sarah Trump said that her sister had left Winsham well before three o'clock in the afternoon and, according to Mrs Mary Rio, she arrived at her shop in the Market Square, Chard at about a quarter-past three. Betty remained in the shop for about half an hour and Mrs Rio could remember the time quite well because the 'Traveller' mail coach had passed on its way to Exeter. At Mr Treasure's shop Betty had bought the plates and was seen by Betsy Batten walking through Crimchard at about four o'clock. John Hutchings noticed the girl passing the George Inn at Combe St Nicholas around half past five, and shortly after, two boys, Richard Fowler and William Coles, saw Betty going up Stoopers Hill towards Buckland St Mary; the two youngsters also confirmed William Flood's statement that he had been muck-spreading. Labourer William Spiller passed her as he walked home down Stoopers Hill at about half past five and judged it would take about a quarter of an hour to reach the crossroads on the Ilminster to Honiton turnpike.

The last two witnesses to confirm a sighting of Betty Trump were James Gothard and William Wilmot. Gothard stated that at about a quarter to six he had been feeding hay to his horse in one of his two fields near Combe Beacon when the young girl had passed him. He recalled that she had been wearing a very light dress and carrying a basket. Gothard stated that he had not spoken to the girl and took no notice of her. He had not known her at the time but had recognised her as Betty Trump after seeing her dead body. William Wilmot stated that he had been working at Combe Beacon all day on 20 February and recollected seeing Betty walk past at about nine o'clock in the morning and returning again that evening as he finished work at about a quarter to six. He knew the time because it took him about a quarter of an hour to walk home to Combe St Nicholas and the church clock struck six as he arrived at his cottage. William Wilmot had been with James Gothard when Betty had passed the two men and he contradicted Gothard's statement that he had taken no notice of the girl. Wilmot stated that Gothard had looked after the girl and commented that she was a fine girl and would make a good sweet-heart. The committee subsequently made enquiries into the contra-dictions of this evidence and it was revealed that although Gothard had been foddering his horse for the night he was met by a Mr Gillet as he rode in the direction Betty Trump had taken. Gothard admitted talking to Mr Gillet but then had gone home to his cottage at Ham, between Combe Beacon and the Ilminster turnpike, where he lived alone. The committee interviewed Gothard at length about his move-ments on the evening of 20 February but the account he gave must have been satisfactory because they took no further action.

The public examination of witnesses began on 28 March and the first to give evidence was Daniel Parsons who recalled that he had found Betty Trump's body with her throat cut in Coppice Burrows. He stated that there was some blood on the ground and a little on her dress but made no mention of disturbed clothing or signs of a struggle. After finding the body he had gone to Grange Farm for help and on his return he found Betty's father and two other men standing by the corpse.

Mr Cox, the attorney, was allowed to cross-examine the witness and, asked about his movements on the evening of the murder, Parsons stated that he was several miles away at a meeting in the Broadway Methodist Chapel. Parsons also took great pains to account for the details of his movements by stating that he was never within half a mile of the murder spot and recalled that as he passed Betty Trump's grandfather's house on the road to Broadway, her grandmother had been at the garden gate and told him that it was half past five. The witness stated that the meeting at the chapel had already started when he arrived at seven o'clock.

Betty's father, Samuel, told how he had found her body and, like Parsons, he described her injuries but made no reference to disturbed clothing or signs of a struggle. In reply to Mr Cox, he stated that Betty had not gone to Sunday School the week before her death, not because, as it had been widely alleged, she was frightened of being molested by the prisoner, but because her two young cousins had come to see her and she had stayed at home to play with them. Samuel Trump went on to say that Betty had never complained to him or anyone else that Flood had behaved improperly to her and she had never expressed a wish not to go to Sunday School.

Mrs Elizabeth Trump recounted her instructions to Betty to go to Winsham and make the purchases on her way home. She stated that all the articles were still in the basket when it was bought back with her body. Cross-examined, Mrs Trump confirmed her husband's statement of the reason why Betty had not gone to Sunday School and that she had never complained about the prisoner's behaviour.

Because the magistrates were due to attend the Somerset Spring Assizes, the further examination of witnesses was adjourned until 7 April when evidence was given by the witnesses who had seen Betty on her last walk.

Having established the timetable, the prosecutors then set out to prove that William Flood had the opportunity to follow and murder the young girl. Miss Honor Marsh of Grange Farm recalled that she had been visiting Edward Churchill at Newtown and a little after six o'clock on the day in question was walking home along the turnpike in the direction of Ilminster. The evening was moonlit and she noticed a figure go over the crossroads from the direction of Combe St Nicholas but could not distinguish whether it was male or female. About a minute or so later, as she neared the crossroads, William Flood came around the corner from Street Ash walking at a normal pace and as they passed, the witness recalled saying, 'So, William, you are going home alone', to which he had replied, 'Yes Miss Marsh, fine weather today.'

Blacksmith John Dommett and his apprentice, Samuel Partridge, testified that they had been working in and about the blacksmith's shop adjoining the Ilminster to Honiton turnpike during the late afternoon of 20 February. At about five o'clock Samuel had been sent to Westhay for some hay and stated that he had returned at about a quarter to six. The blacksmith and his apprentice had weighed it and put it up into the stable loft. This took about ten minutes and then Dommett and the boy went to collect the blacksmith's horse from a field nearly half a mile away. John Dommett estimated that this had taken roughly half an hour and they had arrived back at about a quarter-past six. He had then gone into his house but did not see William Flood pass at any time. Samuel Partridge stated that he had groomed the horse but because it had been very dirty this had taken over three-quarters of an hour. He recalled seeing William Flood pass the blacksmith's shop not long after they arrived back, and when he had finished grooming the horse he had gone into his master's house. Samuel did not know what time he had finished but he recalled that about half an hour later he heard the blacksmith's clock strike eight.

The evidence of the blacksmith and his apprentice was seized upon by the magistrates because it indicated that William Flood had passed the shop at about seven o'clock and therefore, as he could not have arrived home at a quarter-past six, he had ample time to have committed the murder

Mr Cox sought to cross-examine the witnesses but he was refused, thereby preventing the submission of crucial information which could have materially affected the veracity their statements. John Dommett, if cross-examined, would have been forced to admit that his clock, which formed the basis on the timing, was always half to three quarters of an hour fast.

Hester Board remembered that on the Thursday evening she had been looking out for the return of her husband, James. Her house faced John Dommett's stable and from her window she could see both ways along the turnpike. She had seen the blacksmith putting the hay into the stable loft but had not seen William Flood walking along the road. However Hester Board admitted that she had put her children to bed and visited her neighbour during the time the accused could have passed her house.

There had been allegations that on the day before Betty Trump's body was found, Mr Thomas Dean of Cotleigh Farm, near Chard, had been hunting on Buckland Hill and when his hounds had approached the wood where the body lay, William Flood had distracted their attention. The evidence given by Mr Dean and Joseph Parsons, his huntsman, was inconclusive and tended to refute the allegations.

The examination of witnesses concluded on 8 April and the magistrates considered that they had established the following case against William Flood.

The accused had followed Betty Trump from Street Ash to the crossroads, where, seeing Miss Marsh, he had momentarily given up the pursuit, but after she had passed he cut across the common to Coppice Burrows and committed the murder. The accused had then returned the same way and was seen passing Dommett's blacksmith's shop at seven o'clock, rather than between a quarter and twenty-five past six. William Hanning Esq., the chairman of the magistrates, told William Flood that he must account for the loss of time between his meeting Miss Marsh and passing the blacksmith's shop nearly one hour later.

Mr Cox interposed at this moment and offered to call seven witnesses, including Mr Samuel Wyatt, his nephew and niece, to prove that William Flood was at New House Farm at twenty minutes past six on the evening of the murder. The magistrates refused on the grounds that the evidence had proved that the accused did not pass the blacksmith's shop until seven o'clock and evidence as to his arrival at home would contradict that testimony. They went on to say that it was not within their province to judge between conflicting evidence.

William Flood protested that the committee had promised that his witnesses would be heard but once again this was refused and he was committed to Ilchester Gaol to await trial at the Summer Assizes charged with the murder and violation of Betty Trump.

On Wednesday 9 April, William Flood was taken from the room at the Green Dragon Inn which had been his prison for over a month, placed in a chaise, and, guarded by the Bow Street runner, Samuel

Taunton, and Hooper, the constable of Combe St Nicholas, was conveyed to Ilchester.

The Gaol Register provides a brief glimpse of William Flood who was described as a fresh complexioned, well built man, 5 feet 7 $^{1}/_{2}$ inches tall, with brown hair, grey eyes and a long nose. William Flood appeared at the Somerset Assizes in Bridgwater on 11 August 1823 when the judge, Sir James Burrough, advised the Grand Jury that although he believed the facts in the case had been sufficient to justify the prisoner's committal, if they were not furnished with further evidence which might, in their opinion, lead to a conviction, it would be prudent not to proceed. The Grand Jury considered that because this evidence was not forthcoming they dismissed the case and William Flood was released.

Following his discharge, William Flood called on William Hanning Esq. and sought to satisfy the magistrate that he was not guilty of the murder but his efforts were in vain. Mr Hanning told him that in his opinion there were many things which remained unexplained and if Flood lived for forty years he would not be able to go to a fair or revel without being called by some nickname or in some way charged with the murder and he, the magistrate, suggested that Flood go to live in America.

Returning to Buckland St Mary with the comments of Mr Hanning ringing in his ears, William Flood was even more anxious to clear his name and put to rest the whispers and gossip. With the help of friends he published a small book stating the facts of the murder and the substance of the depositions taken before the magistrates. Also included was the evidence which would have been put forward in his defence if the case had gone to trial and would have confirmed that he had passed along the turnpike between six o'clock and a quarter-past, details of his arrival home, and information about a stranger being seen on the road near Coppice Burrows at about the time the murder took place and an unknown horseman seen galloping from the direction of Buckland Hill towards Combe St Nicholas. Also mentioned were the doubts expressed by many people who had seen the place of the murder that the body could not have lain there from Thursday to Sunday.

The book also included certificates signed by many of the principal farmers and inhabitants of Buckland St Mary declaring that they believed William Flood to be innocent. The murder of Betty Trump was never solved and no one else, it seems, other than William Flood was suspected of the crime. However, on 24 August 1835, the following letter appeared in the *Sherborne Journal*:

To the Editor,

Dear Penny, Probably you remember the circumstances of the violation and murder of the young woman of the name of Elizabeth Trump on Buckland Hill some years ago and that a man of the name of William Flood was apprehended and committed to Ilchester Gaol on suspicion of being the perpetrator of both crimes but that the Grand Jury at the Bridgwater Assize following, ignored the Bill preferred against him. From a short time after the latter period, Flood came to reside with a widowed sister at Nether Ham for the purpose of managing a little farm which she occupied there, and subsequently became the occupier himself through his sister's resignation in his favour. His conduct (with exception of having latterly cohabited with a widow woman, whom, it is now evident that he had made arrangements for marrying as soon as he had recovered his health) during his residence at Ham, has been exemplary in the extreme. Labouring for some years past under organic disease of the heart and the large blood vessels, his disease all at once, as it were, assumed the most threatening aspect and the persons about him were in momentary expectation of his death. In this state of things on Saturday last, I was called to him, and feeling it more particularly my duty in this case than in instances where charges and imputation of such grave and momentous nature had not been cast upon the character and conduct of the individual sinking into eternity before me, I confirmed, immediately the apprehensions and anticipations of himself and those around him. The most perfect resignation that a dying Christian could display, preceded and followed the prognostication, and desiring, as probably the last opportunity he might have of doing so, and perhaps the most benefiting one for such an undertaking, (being about to receive the Holy Sacrament within the next hour), to leave behind him the most convincing declaration he could then make of his innocence of, or connection with, the charges of violation and murder, I, at his request, drew up the annexed form, to which he subscribed his name in my presence and in the presence of other persons who were in the room. The poor fellow lingered until morning asserting and protesting his innocence to the last.

Believe me to remain ever your

William Norman

Langport August 25, 1835

Annex

I, William Flood believing that my end is fast approaching and that I shall shortly appear before Him from whom no secrets are hid, declare solemnly, and as it were my dying breath, that I am entirely innocent of the foul charge of murder, of which I have been accused, and that I know nothing whatever relating to the commission or contemplation of the dreadful deed.

(Signed) William Flood
Witness, Wm Norman, Surgeon
Nether Ham 22nd August, 1835

William Flood was interred in High Ham churchyard on 29 August 1835, number 350 in the burial register.

'I AM FREE AND INNOCENT OF THE CRIME!'

William Guppy, who supplemented his labourer's wage with a little horse dealing at Touchays, near Chard, was at his cottage door one day in March 1829, discussing his favourite sideline with John Russell and Charles Tytherly, two lace-makers. Suddenly Russell exclaimed, 'Look there, here's a pretty bitch coming down the lane!' and pointed to the neat figure of Joan Turner walking towards them.

'Why what's the cause?' enquired Guppy.

'That little bitch had out a summons against I and another for making work with her, and I got charged 5 shillin' by the magistrate. When I do get the chance I'll give her a sly pat,' John Russell replied. As the young woman passed and disappeared along the road no one could know that this conversation would be recalled twelve months later when John Russell was on trial for his life.

Tuesday, the first day of December, 1829, dawned windy and mild over Chard and as she walked to work in the early morning, Harriet White found a woman's body lying near the path leading from Lower Touchays up the Six Acre field to Avishayes Lane. Squealing with fear, Harriet turned and fled back down the path to Jacob and Joan Summers who were following a little way behind. Throwing her arms around Joan Summer's neck, she blurted out the terrible find. Jacob ran up the path but even in the dim light of a winter morning, the bloody and disarranged clothes were enough to tell him what had probably happened. For a moment Summers could not make out the features of the corpse but then to his horror he recognised the dead woman as Joan Turner who lodged at Touchays and worked at Riste's Mill Lane lace factory in Chard. He could also see that her throat had been cut, her pettycoats were pulled up to her stomach and there was blood smeared over her thighs. In an unconscious effort to preserve some modesty for the dead woman, Jacob Summers pulled the pettycoats down over the bloody thighs and re-arranged her clothes.

Leaving his wife and the trembling Harriet White to guard the body Summers ran to Chard and, arriving at the bottom of Fore Street, he shouted, 'Murder, Murder, Murder!' Within moments he was joined by half a dozen men, including factory owner Benjamin Richards, and they followed him back to the scene of the crime. A short discussion took place and the townsmen returned to Chard to raise the authorities and spread the word, leaving Jacob Summers to stand guard.

As he waited, Summers heard the eight o'clock breakfast bell ring from Riste's factory and shortly after workers and more townspeople began to arrive in the field, followed by the Chard parish overseer who sent for a cart to convey the body of Joan Turner to the workhouse.

Surgeon Northcote Spicer was called to examine the dead woman and he found that repeated cuts and slashes to her throat had severed her windpipe and carotid artery. Joan's jacket had been slashed several times close to the right shoulder but although there was the mark of a bloody hand on her left thigh and smears of blood on the right, there were no signs of a sexual assault. The immediate suspect was laceworker, John Russell, whose previous conduct towards Joan Turner was common knowledge. Joseph Salisbury and Robert Norris, two of the Chard town constables, went to Riste's factory, and took Russell in custody to the workhouse.

Robert Salisbury then went to the Six Acre field which he searched thoroughly but although there was some blood splattered in this field and in the one to the west adjoining Stephen's Lane, no weapon was found.

On the constable's return, the questioning of Russell began. He denied all knowledge of the murder and readily gave a statement of his movements on the previous evening. Russell told the town officers that, in company with Thomas Harp, he had left Riste's factory when it closed at eight o'clock and had gone to Harp's home at Furnham on the Ilminster road to collect some leeks and greens. He had returned home at about half past eight, had a bit of supper, and because there was only a small piece of candle left in the house, he and his wife and baby had gone to bed. Russell went on to say that he had nursed his infant son for some of the night. On his way back from Thomas Harp's he recalled that he had passed several people and boys on the road, but as the night was very dark he had not recognised anyone although he had wished one man goodnight.

John Russell repeated his story when examined by the Vicar of Chard, the Reverend A.B. Whitehead, who was one of the town magistrates, adding that he had been drinking with Thomas Harp and his father William last Sunday evening and as he had had a little drop too much he had fallen in some mud. Russell also admitted that he had been summonsed for an assault on the deceased over a year before but since then she had not complained about his behaviour.

Thomas and William Harp were brought to the workhouse and repeatedly questioned by the town officials and magistrates. Both confirmed that Russell had collected the leeks and greens but they had no knowledge of the murder until it became known in the factory and in the town.

Surgeon Northcote Spicer was called to examine Russell and, although his clothes were not blood-stained, he noted some small scratches on Russell's face which he thought might have been made by small fingers, possibly in play. At about eleven o'clock on the Tuesday morning, another Chard constable, Francis Mayo, accompanied by Surgeon Spicer, searched Russell's house which was in a court next to Furnham House and east of the junction of the Ilminster and Crewkerne turnpike roads. Here they found a shirt which was damp on the breast and on the sleeves, from the cuffs to the elbows, and a damp waistcoat. A pair of partly dry black stockings were hung up on the wall behind the kitchen door. The garments were closely examined for signs of blood but none were found and a thorough search of the house produced nothing incriminating. The only other trousers Russell owned were unmarked.

The first of December also saw the arrival of the coroner, Mr Caines, who opened his inquiries and, with the assistance of the town magistrates and constables, these went on for three days. During this time John Russell was kept in close custody in the workhouse and despite being constantly questioned, he continued to protest his innocence and did not depart from his first account.

Whilst Russell was held in the workhouse, Constable Norris questioned his wife Jane, and she confirmed that her husband had come home a little after the factory bell had rung. He had picked up a bag and said that he was going to Furnham for some greens. As he left, Jane said that she had called out for him not to stay long as she had some potatoes boiling and they would soon be done. Her husband had returned about twenty minutes later, had his supper and, because there was only a small piece of candle left, they had gone to bed just after nine o'clock. Jane Russell went on to say that they had stayed in bed until the first factory bell rang on the Tuesday morning. (This bell rang at 6.20 am and again at 6.40 a.m.)

The inquest into the death of Joan Turner was held on Thursday 3 December and the jury returned a verdict of 'Wilful Murder against some person or persons unknown.' John Russell was released as there was insufficient evidence to continue to hold him in custody and he went home.

Joan Turner had come to Chard from Marshwood, but her body would not be returned to the village overlooking the beautiful Vale which takes its name, and on 5 December 1829, at the age of twenty-two years, she was laid to rest in the churchyard at Chard.

The town of Chard and the countryside around continued to seethe with excitement and speculation. Hundreds of curious spectators visited the Six Acre field to gawp at the bloody marks where Joan Turner met her untimely end and it was reported that the land soon became a sea of mud.

John Russell went back to his lacemaking machine at Riste's factory but not to peace of mind. The murder of Joan Turner continued to be the main topic of conversation and Russell continued to be the main suspect. He was pointed out in the street and asked about the murder by neighbours and acquaintances. Everyday he ran the gauntlet of whispers and innuendoes and to make matters worse for him, a committee of local gentry and businessmen, set up after the inquest, were questioning workmates, neighbours and friends. To all who would listen, John Russell continued to protest his innocence and repeat his alibi.

The committee of inquiry offered a reward of £100, a small fortune in 1829, for the discovery of the murderer and were soon piecing together a chain of circumstantial evidence against their prime suspect, John Russell. History is silent on the reason for this relentless pursuit of Russell. Certainly he would appear to have been a drinking man of dubious morals and possibly not a very good husband to Jane Larcombe, whom he married in July, 1829, but this character reference could have applied to many other men of Chard at the time. The charge against him for 'making work' with Joan Turner had involved lifting her pettycoats in the hay and another man, called Quick, had been an accomplice in this minor indiscretion.

Whatever the reason, the evidence was coming together. The light of a large fire had been observed coming from Russell's kitchen in the early morning of 1 December, the pump of the well in the yard behind his house was said to have been worked at the same time, and blood-stained water was seen in the trough to the pump. Russell's shirt and waistcoat had been found to be damp, he was observed to have been unusually clean when he arrived at work on the Tuesday morning and enquiries at the factory disclosed that he had mentioned the murder before anyone could have known about it. However the murder weapon had not been found and, as matters turned out, never would be.

On Saturday 21 December, the town magistrates considered that enough evidence had been placed before them to warrant Russell's arrest on suspicion of murdering Joan Turner, and he was taken into custody to Ilchester Gaol to await trial at the Somerset Lent Assizes. The Ilchester Gaol description book provides our only impression of John Russell. He is described as being 23 years of age, standing 5 feet 4 inches tall, slightly built with an oval face, dark brown hair and hazel eyes. There was a scar on his forehead over his left eye and a cut on the thumb of his left hand. The prisoner was born in Crewkerne, had originally been a baker by trade, was married with one child and could read but not write – a very average looking chap, but then suspected murderers usually are.

With Russell lodged in gaol his income ceased and as his wife could no longer pay the rent of their modest house, she was evicted and, because her husband was a native of Crewkerne, she was despatched with her baby to the Crewkerne workhouse to prevent them becoming a burden on the ratepayers of Chard.

Now that the house was empty, a further inspection was carried out by the Chard constables, accompanied by Surgeons Spicer and Ware, and more damning evidence came to light when blood spots were found on the stair case and in the bedroom.

John Russell was brought before Mr Justice Gaselee at eight o'clock on the morning of Wednesday 7 April 1830 at the assizes in Taunton. The courtroom was packed to capacity to hear the prisoner in a firm voice plead 'not guilty my lord' to the murder of Joan Turner on 30 November 1829 with 'some sharp instrument.'

The prosecution was led by Mr Follett with Mr William Erle defending and as events were to prove, John Russell's defence could have been in no better hands. William Erle had a reputation for the thorough way in which he handled his cases and he was to achieve high judicial office and a knighthood. He was a Dorset man, born at Fifehead Magdalen near Gillingham in 1793, and was described as appearing like a country gentleman with a fresh and ruddy complexion and speaking with a slight Dorset accent.

In the 1830s a trial at the Assizes would be opened by a speech from the prosecuting counsel who would then call witnesses to prove his case. When the prosecution's case had been presented, the accused could make a speech in his own defence but his counsel was not allowed to speak on behalf of his client. The defence, however, could call witnesses and cross-examine the prosecution's (who could in turn cross-examine those appearing for the defence).

Opening the case for the prosecution, Mr Follett stated that the evidence was principally of a circumstantial nature and then proceeded to tell the jury that on the evening of Monday 30 November 1829, Joan Turner had left the lace factory where she worked at eight o'clock to walk to her lodgings at Touchays. She had been in company with a little girl called Mary Ann Carter as far as Stephens Lane and before the deceased took her leave, her small companion had heard a man jump over a nearby hedge into the road. At nine o'clock a scream was heard from the direction of the field in which the body of Joan Turner was found. The rear of the prisoner's house was visible from Furnham House and, on the night of the murder, two servants heard the pump in the nearby yard working and saw a light in the prisoner's home and his wife walking about the room. The next morning the house was searched and a shirt found to be wet on the breast and sleeves. Some neighbours going to the pump saw some bloody water which had not been there on the preceding evening. The prisoner had scratches on his face when first taken into custody and several weeks later some blood was found on the floor of his house. The body was discovered on the 1 December but this fact was not told to the workers coming from Riste's factory until after the eight o'clock bell had rung yet the prisoner had mentioned the murder to some persons in the factory before that time. It was also necessary to tell the jury that there had been some previous quarrel between the deceased and the prisoner.

Mr Follett then called his first witness, Harriet White, who recalled how she had found the body. Jacob Summers followed and recounted how he had seen and recognised the dead woman and had run into Chard to raise the alarm. The witness said that he had only shouted 'murder' a few times before he was joined by Mr Benjamin Richards and several other men. They had not stayed in the town but had returned immediately to Six Acre field. Summers remembered hearing the eight o'clock bell ring from Riste's factory whilst he remained guarding the corpse and shortly afterwards workpeople began to arrive in the field.

Medical evidence was given by the surgeon, Northcote Spicer, who stated that at nine o'clock on the Tuesday morning he had been called to examine the body of Joan Turner at the workhouse. He found a deep wound which commenced a little below the left ear behind the angle of the jaw and continued a little downward across the throat into the windpipe. The wound was not inflicted by one cut but by many repeated cuts. The principal blood vessels were divided and this had caused death. Surgeon Spicer also found two long cuts through the clothes over the right shoulder but these had only slightly cut the skin. He went on to describe how 'the surface of the bowels and both thighs were covered in blood, as if a hand had been wiped over them.' The surgeon considered that the wounds were inflicted with a sharp pointed knife, but not a 'good cutting knife.' There were no signs of a struggle prior to the wounds being inflicted and no indication of any indecent assault.

Surgeon Spicer then stated that he had examined the prisoner on the morning he was brought into custody and noticed some scratches on his face. Cross-examined by Mr Erle, the surgeon agreed that these were such that might have resulted from a playful scuffle and more resembled the pressure of a small nail rather than a scratch. To establish the time of the murder Mr Follett now called John Bragg who said that he could see the Six Acre field from his house about half a mile away. He had heard three terrible screams coming from the direction of the field some ten minutes after his son came home just after half past eight on the evening of 30 November.

Cross-examined, the witness stated that he had been told about the murder during the following morning but as he had been ill he had not been able to go to the inquest. Although he had mentioned the screams to many people, he had not reported it to the magistrates because he had not been asked to do so; however he had told Norris, the town constable.

Fifteen-year-old Elias England, the next witness, said that he had been walking home with his brother from Riste's factory along Avishayes Lane and, as they neared the Six Acre field, they heard the Town Hall clock strike nine. At that moment someone jumped over a nearby hedge and shortly after the boys heard some low groans coming from the field. The sounds frightened them and they ran home as fast as they could. Cross-examined, Elias stated that he had heard no screams.

Robert Bragg, aged twelve, stated that he was employed at Riste's factory and on 30 November he had left work at about ten minutes past eight. He recalled that as he walked along the Ilminster road towards his home at Furnham, he saw John Russell standing by the milestone and shortly after the prisoner, in company with another man, had overtaken him.

Ten-year-old Mary Ann Carter was the last human being, other than the murderer, to see Joan Turner alive. Mary Ann told the court that she had left Riste's factory with Joan at about eight o'clock and they had walked hand in hand to Mr Chapman's shop where Joan bought a loaf of bread. As they left Chapman's the child recalled that, 'Joan Turner took my hand again and did not let it go until I had got as far as Stephens Lane which leads to Furnham from Avishayes Lane. I heard a man jump in Stephens Lane and I said, 'Joan, what's that?' and she said ,'My dear, nothing that will hurt you'. It seemed to be a man with hobnails in his shoes. I don't know on which side he jumped and I heard someone go up Avishayes Lane. Joan then left me and said, 'Good night my dear,' and I went to my home. I don't know whether she went up Avishayes Lane or across the fields. There is a footpath across them which leads to her house.' Cross-examined by Mr Erle, Mary Ann said that she heard no screams at any time after she left Joan Turner and went home to Furnham along Stephens Lane.

Joseph Salisbury, one of the Chard constables, next entered the witness box and stated that after taking John Russell into custody he had searched the Six Acres and the adjoining field. The body had been removed by the time he carried out the search but although he had found several spots of blood, he had found no weapon. The constable then recounted the statement made by the prisoner when he was taken into custody on 1 December and stated that Russell had confirmed that the shoes he was wearing were the same as those he wore on the previous evening. The witness noted that there were hobnails in them. Cross-examined, Joseph Salisbury agreed that the prisoner had readily answered all the questions put to him.

Chard constable, Robert Norris, now gave evidence and corroborated that given by Joseph Salisbury and added that one of the bloody marks in the field appeared as if a man had wiped a blood-drenched arm. Norris stated that the prisoner's wife had confirmed that her husband had returned home at about a quarter to nine and had not gone out again.

The next witness, Susan Dinham, said that she was a servant of Mrs Clarke of Furnham House and on 30 November the household consisted of her mistress, Sarah Carter and herself, and George Edwards. She recalled that Mrs Clarke had been away on the night in question and both serving girls had gone to bed at half past ten. The room she shared with Sarah Carter overlooked the prisoner's house and she had noticed a light in his kitchen window. Susan went on to say that at about two or three o'clock in the morning she had been woken up by the sound of the pump being worked in the adjoining yard. She had got up and looked out and saw a light coming from the Russell's kitchen window. After about 5 minutes the servant went back to bed and the pump was still working when she finally dropped off to sleep. When Susan got up at daybreak, just before the first factory bell rang, she had looked out again and this time saw a great light coming from the prisoner's window and a woman, whom she presumed was Russell's wife, walking backwards and forwards wearing her everyday dress.

Susan Dinham further testified that she had cleaned the prisoner's house, which was owned by Mrs Clarke, the day before he took occupation and about a month before the murder and there were no spots of blood on the staircase or in the only bedroom.

The second servant, Sarah Carter, confirmed that a light was showing in the prisoner's kitchen window when she had gone to bed and also when she got up the following morning between four and five o'clock. However she had not been aware of Susan Dinham getting up in the night and she had not heard the pump working.

The next witness was eighty-year-old Hannah Wire who lived next door to the Russells. She explained that the pump in the yard behind her house was shared by several families and on 30 November she had gone to bed sometime after nine o'clock. She did not go to the pump during that night but when she went to it at about half past seven the following morning she saw some bloody water in the trough and in the gutter running to the privy. The old lady also noticed two whiting heads floating in the trough, but these, she said, were very white.

Neighbour James Morris was the next witness who stated that between five and six o'clock on the Monday evening he had cleaned two whiting at the trough. There was no blood in the fish and he did not use the pump again that night. Another neighbour, Maria Perram, described the layout of the houses. She said that there was a yard at the back surrounded by a high wall and a passageway led from the street. The door to the passage was usually locked at half past nine at night and some of the houses, including the prisoner's, had no door to the street and could only be entered from the back yard. She stated that she had not used the pump on the night of 30 November.

Mary Peadon, Hannah Wire's daughter, was the next witness. She confirmed that her mother had gone to bed just after nine o'clock and then she had supper with her husband. At about half past nine she placed a candle in her back window and went out to the privy. Some five minutes later as she was going back across the yard she heard the sound of a quarrel coming from the prisoner's house. Although Mary listened for a few moments she could not hear what was being said, but she thought there were more than two people involved.

The witness then recounted a conversation she had with John Russell on the day he was released from custody following his first arrest. The prisoner said that he had seen the candle in the back window when he came home at about half past eight. Mary Peadon told him that he was wrong, because the candle had not been put there until half past nine. At that moment the witness stated that William Long, who lodged with the Peadons, came in and, when asked, he confirmed that the candle had been in the window when he came home just after ten o'clock. Mary Peadon recalled that the prisoner then suggested that if she was asked to give evidence about the time the candle was in the window she would agree with him but, she told the court, that she had refused. The witness also stated that she did not go to the pump during the night and did not get up until eight o'clock on the Tuesday morning.

William Long confirmed Mary Peadon's evidence and said that he had remained in his room all night on 30 November One by one the people who lived in the adjoining dwellings testified that they had not used the pump during the night of the murder and William Boobier stated that he had locked the door to the passage at eleven o'clock and gone to bed.

The owner of the prisoner's house, Mrs Clarke, testified that he had taken occupation early in November 1829, and about a fortnight after the murder she had gone to the property, for a reason she did not specify and had seen some marks on the top of the stairs and in the bedroom which appeared to be spots of blood. She stated that they had not been there when she had been in the house before Russell took possession.

Francis Mayo, another of the Chard constables, followed Mrs Clarke into the witness box. He recounted how he had gone to the house at eleven o'clock on the morning of 1 December and, in the bedroom, he had found a shirt with the breast and sleeves partly wet and a damp, light-coloured waistcoat. In the kitchen he had found a pair of partly-dried black, worsted stockings hanging on a line behind the door.

Cross-examined by Mr Erle, the constable stated that he only found one pair of trousers in the house and there were no marks on them. He had searched the house most thoroughly but did not see any spots of blood on the staircase or in the bedroom. However, the floors were dirty and he admitted that he had been more interested in inspecting clothes than floors. Mayo went on to say that the damp shirt smelt as if it had been under a child and the prisoner's wife had told him that the baby had been wrapped in it all night.

The constable recalled going to the house again on Christmas Eve and examining the staircase by the light of a candle. He had found spots of blood both on the stairs and on the walls as if shaken from a bloody hand. More blood spots were found under the bed when it was moved. The next witness, Aaron Loveridge, stated that he had worked with the prisoner at Riste's factory and at about a quarter to eight on the morning the murder was discovered, he noticed that Russell was unusually neat and tidy. He was wearing a clean shirt, neckcloth and trousers and newly blacked shoes. Under cross examination, the witness admitted that he could not say whether he had seen the prisoner on the day before and agreed that Russell regularly changed his neckcloth.

The surgeon, Northcote Spicer, was recalled by the prosecution, and confirmed that he had inspected the prisoner's clothes when he visited the prisoner's house on 1 December. The sleeves of the shirt were uniformly wet to the elbows but only the front was damp. He observed no smell and was of the opinion that the shirt was damp from washing because if it had been under a child it would only be wet in places.

The surgeon stated that he had gone to the house again just before Christmas and examined the spots of blood. There were spots on the third and fifth stairs, splashes against the side partition on the second and third stairs and a great number in the bedroom near the top of the staircase. The spots resembled blood mingled with water rather than blood itself and appeared to have been dropped from bloody clothes. He was of the opinion that they could not have been there for more than a few weeks and some appeared more recent than others, going by the amount of dirt on the floor. The surgeon pointed out that the roads had been very muddy at the time of the murder.

Cross-examined by Mr Erle, Northcote Spicer admitted that he had found no blood on the prisoner's woollen clothes, and none had been washed before he examined them. However, he had examined the wet shirt minutely and although he could find no signs of blood or soap being used in the washing, he stated that he had frequently washed out blood-soiled linen without soap. In reply to a further question from Mr Erle, the surgeon recalled finding blood stains in the prisoner's bed.

The last witness of the day was Thomas Hayball, a carpenter, who testified that there were no blood spots on the floor when he had prepared the house for Russell's occupation. The trial which had lasted for nearly twelve hours was adjourned to the following morning. At eight o'clock precisely on 8 April, the court reconvened, and the first witness was local builder, Simeon Stuckey, whose brutal and unsolved murder four months later would cause a further sensation. The builder produced a model of the prisoner's house to prove that the kitchen window could only be seen from the servants' bedroom in Furnham House and from none of the adjoining premises.

Surveyor, William Summers, followed Stuckey and produced a plan which showed that there was no turnpike road from Furnham to Avishayes Lane. He stated that the residence of the deceased was upwards of a mile from the Chard town hall in Fore Street and the path where she was found was *out of the direction of her house*. [Author's italics] This disclosure and its possible implications that Joan Turner had an assignation with someone does not seem to have been questioned by the defence. Joan's conversation with Mary Ann Carter, when the unknown man jumped over the hedge, also indicates that she might have been meeting a man.

Benjamin Richards was called and stated that he lived in Fore Street, Chard and owned a rope and sail cloth factory. He recalled that he had left his home a little after half past seven on the morning of 1 December and was walking down Fore Street to his factory when he saw a group of men clustered around Jacob Summers. They called to him that there had been a murder at the Six Acre field and he joined them as they followed Summers to the scene of the the crime. Richards stated that after viewing the body they had all hurried back to Chard leaving Summers to guard the corpse. When he arrived at the corner of Fore Street and Silver Street it was just after eight o'clock and he met workers from Riste's factory going for their breakfasts. The witness recalled that when he told them of the murder, no one seemed to know about it and during his walk along Silver Street towards the factory everyone he met seemed unaware of the tragedy. As Benjamin Richards passed the factory gate he saw the time keeper, Robert Hutchings who, when told of the murder, also expressed ignorance of the deed. The witness hurried on to the Chard workhouse, and after reporting the murder to the overseer, returned home at about half past eight.

Robert Hutchings, the factory time-keeper, stated that he lived in the porter's lodge and rang the first bell of the day at twenty minutes past six, and the second at twenty minutes to seven. The bell rang again at eight o'clock for the main body of workpeople to go to breakfast and at twenty minutes past eight for the rest to go. No-one could leave the factory before eight o'clock without a ticket and no-one had gone out on the morning of 1 December. When Mr Richards told him of the murder, he looked at the clock and it was about a quarter past eight.

The factory clerk, Robert Gawler, the next witness, recalled that he was in the counting house when Robert Hutchings told him about the murder at a quarter-past eight. He could remember the time because the time-keeper had then gone and rung the twenty past eight factory bell. He confirmed that neither he nor Thomas Riste, the owner's son, had given any tickets of leave before eight o'clock that morning. The clerk explained that 450 people worked in the factory and 350 went to breakfast at eight o' clock, leaving 100 to work the machines and they would go to breakfast between twenty and half past eight when the others returned. Gawler stated that if a lace worker had not finished the piece he was making, he would remain at his machine until it was done, and then go to breakfast. The boys who helped the lacemakers would be sent to breakfast at eight o'clock even if the piece their master was working on had not been finished. Thomas Riste confirmed that he had not issued any tickets before eight o'clock on 1 December.

The evidence given by the following witnesses who worked in the factory was crucial to the prosecution in seeking to establish Russell's guilt beyond reasonable doubt; so far the evidence had been very circumstantial. To better understand the production of lace and the operations mentioned by the work people, the following account is given in *Chard in 1851* by Chard History Group.

Chard Lace was 'plain net' or 'bobbin net', machine made and bearing no resemblance to the hand-made Honiton 'pillow' lace. It was simple, plain, wide netting, usually without any pattern. It was in great demand for net curtains, for mosquito nets, for trimming on ladies hats and dresses and for undergarments.

Production involved various stages:

1. Hank-to-bobbin Winding. The yarn came direct from the Manchester spinners by waggon, usually in hank form. It was slipped loosely onto a free-running spoken frame, and drawn off by girls or women through a guide onto wooden bobbins.

2. Brass Bobbin Winding. A large number of these wooden bobbins were then placed in a rack and drawn off through guides into brass bobbins. These were finely made, and comprised a slim circular brass bobbin, 37mm diameter and only 1.5mm thick, revolving inside a slender case. Winding these, too, was a female occupation, carried on near the lace machines themselves.

3. Threading. The brass bobbins were then fitted in a closely

packed line in a bobbin carriage, ready for insertion in the lace machine. The yarn from each bobbin had to be threaded through an eyelet – a tedious job, usually done by boys (*in the brass room*).

4. Warping. A long rack was filled with a line of up to 200 wooden bobbins. Their threads were drawn off, through guides to converge in groups onto a drum. From this the 'groups' of threads were wound off onto a 'beam' (in fact a long roller). The beam was then carried to the lace machine, and placed in position. Obviously this involved heavy lifting and so warping was usually done by men.

5. Making. Usually one 'twist hand' or 'lace hand', with a boy, looked after a pair of large machines. His was a skilled job. He began by setting the machine up. He untied a bundle of warp threads, and led them from the beam through various guides to the net roller at the other end of the machine. Eventually, when all the threads were connected to the net roller in this way, and had been tensioned, the warp was ready. The brass bobbin carriages were then set into slots in the machine. Once the heavy machine began working, the twist hand had to watch intently. If a thread broke it had to be repaired immediately. The bobbins had to be lubricated with thinly sprinkled black graphite, as grease would spoil the the yarn (so, making the white lace was a surprisingly dirty job – *and why Aaron Loveridge's comments about Russell's clean shirt etc was considered so pertinent*).

The operations of Mending, Packing and Maintenance are not described because they have no relevance to the evidence given by the lace workers.

George Gillett was the first of the lace workers to take the stand and he stated that his machine was next to John Russell's. He recollected that he saw the prisoner working his machine before 7 am on 1 December but could not be definite as to the exact time when Russell first told him of the murder but believed it was before 8 am even though the factory bell could not be heard over the noise of the machines and he had no watch. The witness stated that the prisoner had told him that a girl had been murdered going across a field near Avishayes. When he enquired whether Russell had seen the girl he had replied that he had not, but would go and see when he went to breakfast. Gillett then asked who she was and the prisoner stated that she was a girl with a squint eye who worked in the factory.

When asked whether she was a short girl, Russell said 'yes' and the witness said that he knew her. Following this conversation, the two men continued to work their machines and shortly after Thomas Harp came into the machine room and spoke to the prisoner. However, Gillett could not hear what was being said and after about twenty minutes he stopped work and went to see the body.

Cross-examined by Mr Erle, Gillett said that he worked at his machine with his back to Russell and it was possible for people to go out and come in without his knowing. Someone might have spoken to the prisoner without him being aware if it. The witness now became very confused and admitted that he had said on one occasion that Russell had told him about the murdered girl at five past eight, on a second occasion at ten past eight, but he had never said it was twenty past eight.

Another lace worker, Henry Fowler, stated that he had been told of the murder by George Gillett at five minutes to eight and he knew this to be the time because the people he saw leaving the factory did so at 8 am.

John Lake testified that he was working at his machine when Henry Fowler told him about the murder and he believed that this was about a quarter before eight because afterwards he heard the bell ring.

William Bragg, another lace worker, said that he had heard of the murder at about twenty past eight, but he did not know who had been killed. Vincent Bird testified that he worked in the machine shop and as he was returning from breakfast at about twenty past eight, William Bragg was standing at the door of his house opposite the factory gate and told him that 'the girl who lives down at Rice's has been found murdered.' When the witness went into the machine shop he saw John Russell working and told him that there was 'a poor girl found down in the field with her throat cut.' He recalled the prisoner replying, 'Poor girl, she'll never be no more.' Vincent Bird then left the machine shop and went to the brass room where he told the foreman, Richard Stephenson. Cross examined, the witness could not remember if he used the expression 'cockeyed girl' when he told the prisoner of the murder. Richard Stephenson, the brass room foreman, confirmed that Vincent Bird had spoken about the murder at twenty minutes after eight.

Now followed Henry Perram, Charles Hill, William Bowditch and Thomas Theaker who testified that Jacob Summers had told them of the murder and that they had gone back with him to the Six Acre field.

The coroner, Mr Caines, read Russell's statement made at the inquest about his movements on the evening of 30 November which also said that Vincent Bird was the first person to tell him of the murder. When asked by the judge whether the statement had been made voluntarily, Mr Caines confirmed that it had.

The next witnesses recalled conversations in the brass room on the morning of 1 December. First was John Wood who said that he overheard Thomas Harp say to the prisoner between seven and eight o'clock that morning, 'What sort of engagement had you last night?' to which Russell replied, 'A damned hot one.' Cross-examined by Mr Erle, Wood said that they were about nine or ten feet away from him and there were two other men in between. He swore that the words were not 'I'll have a damned lot of them', and that he did not make a mistake. Harp and the prisoner might have said more but if they did, he had not heard it. Wood admitted, however, that he had found 'in the course of my life, that my ears have misled me.'

The next witness, Robert Hebditch, testified that he was in the brass room on 1 December, and heard Thomas Harp say to the prisoner, 'Well Jack, what engagement were you in last night?' He did not hear the reply. John Rendall, the boy who worked for the prisoner, recalled that on the Monday, Russell had said to him that he was 'going to have a damned, bloody good battle by and by, after I leave work,' and when asked who with, he had replied that he would be 'going fighting along with a bitch.'

Cross-examined by Mr Erle, the boy said that he took care of the prisoner's machine when he went to meals. On 1 December he had gone to breakfast at twenty minutes after eight, leaving Russell at the machine. He had heard nothing about the murder until he left the factory. Rendall revealed that when he had been examined by the coroner he had not told of the conversation on the Monday. He had first mentioned it on the Wednesday of the week before the trial but the boy said that he had told his mother when Russell was arrested. He also stated that the conversation had taken place on the Monday morning after which he had gone to breakfast leaving Russell at the machine.

Mr Erle recalled Robert Hebditch who said that he was working in the brass room on the Monday morning but could not recall seeing the prisoner in the factory.

John Balch testified that he worked in the machine shop and remembered talking to John Russell a week after he had been released from custody. When he had enquired how he had 'got on up there and why he could not set himself free before?' the prisoner had replied, 'I could, if I was innocent.' Russell had gone on to say that one after another people had come in telling stories against him and how he had contradicted what was said. However there was one person who when he came in had made him 'shake.' The prisoner did not reveal who this was but he picked up a spindle and letting it drop said that 'he thought his life was as near gone as that.'

Cross-examined, Joseph Balch stated that Russell might have said that if some of the witnesses had their way his life would have been gone. However, when re-examined by Mr Follett, the witness did not think his last answer was what the prisoner had really said.

Henry Priddle, a former inmate of Ilchester Gaol, was called next and said that last January he had been employed to take care of the prisoner. In one conversation, Russell had told him that on the Monday evening he had been in Harp's garden after some greens and a handfull of leeks. He had taken the greens under one arm and the leeks under the other and had gone home across the Baptist meeting yard and over the wall to his back door.

Robert Mills, a shoe maker, told of seeing the prisoner near the Guildhall and overhearing someone say to him, 'They have accused thee of the murder aren't they?' and he had replied, 'Yes, they have and they shall have a damned hard job to get it out of me, and a damned sight harder to hang me.' Cross-examined, the witness said that it was 'a common thing in Chard to swear.'

Mr John Gunn, the minister of Chard Congregational Church, took the stand and stated that he had been asked by the prisoner to visit him after he had been taken into custody on the second occasion. The minister asked Russell why he had sent for him, and if it was to make a confession, he had begged the prisoner not to make it to him. Mr Gunn said that he had spoken to the prisoner about the awful situation in which he stood and recounted how the man had wept and said, 'God knows I have sins enough to answer for without this murder.' However, Russell continued to maintain his innocence.

John Atherley, another lace worker, followed the minister into the witness box, and recalled a conversation with the prisoner before he was arrested. Russell had asked Atherley whether he thought a murderer could be saved and he had replied that he thought murderers and the worst characters could be saved by repentance. The prisoner then said that if he had not done the murder he had no occasion to fear. On the following day Russell had asked the witness whether he thought it possible for Conjurer Baker (a Devonshire 'wizard', well known in the area in the 1820s and reputed to have powers of second sight) to bring the murderer to light? Atherley did not think this was possible, although there were many wonderful things done in the olden times. After a short pause the prisoner had exclaimed, 'Well I've not committed the murder and by that means I've no guilt on my conscience!'

William Guppy, the part time horse dealer from Touchays, recalled the conversation of twelve months before and Charles Tytherly told of the prisoner's constant talk about Joan Turner. Sarah Legg testified that she had assisted the prisoner's wife during her confinement in August 1829 and stated that there were bloody marks left in the middle of the family's bed.

Joseph Cornelius stated that he lived on the Ilminster road and for several nights before 30 November, Joan Turner had been sleeping at his house as she had been attending his brother who had been ill. The witness did not say whether Joan had intended spending the night of 30 November at his house.

The prisoner's brother, George, now entered the witness box and stated that he had mended a pair of John's shoes on the Friday before the murder and had put clamps on the toes and a few hobs on the soles. He confirmed that the coat, waistcoat, trousers and shoes worn by his brother on the Monday were the same as he wore on the Tuesday he was arrested. George Russell also confirmed that his brother only possessed one coat.

Following two good character references, the trial came to an end and it was time for Mr Justice Gaselee to sum up. He had just begun, when one of the jurymen interrupted and said that they did not want to trouble his Lordship to go further because they had already made up their minds and wished to give a verdict. The learned judge, in a mild rebuke to the jury, told them that this was a case of much doubt and difficulty, and as it required their deepest deliberation it was their duty to go through the evidence. The jury then asked to know more precisely the difference of time between the prisoner mentioning the murder at the factory and it being known in the town. Mr Justice Gaselee continued with his summing up and repeated in detail the evidence given about the conversations in the factory on the morning of the murder.

After consulting for about ten minutes the jury returned a verdict of 'Guilty' to the murder of Joan Turner. John Russell was asked if he had anything to say before judgement to die was passed upon him and for the first time, other than to plead not guilty, he spoke. 'My Lord, what I have to say is this. I am free and innocent of the crime, so help me God. I am happy to leave this life and to meet my God under the circumstances I am now placed in.' He then repeated what he had said in his statement and added that during the Monday night, his wife had gone down to the kitchen to get something for the child. In conclusion John Russell pleaded that he was 'Wholly innocent and know nothing more of the murder than a sucking child, and the Almighty will find it out and the world will know that I am innocent!'

Mr Justice Gaselee then passed sentence of death and ordered that the condemned man should be executed on the coming Saturday and his body given to the surgeons to be dissected and anatomized. When the awful sentence had been delivered John Russell fell to his knees crying out, 'My Lord, you have passed sentence of death on an innocent man!' He was hauled to his feet and taken from the dock.

On Good Friday, 9 April 1830, local diarist Arthur Hull recorded that: 'Russell is condemned to Die his trial last 3 days (sic) he not confessed a word.' On Sunday 11 April he wrote: 'J. Russell to be hanged yesterday but his Council will not give it up and so respite longer.' Arthur Hull then remarked that 'John Russell has taken his trial at Taunton and is condemned to die for the murder of Joan Turner of Chard his Councillor thinking the evidence not sufficient therefore determined to respite his life till a future day. – Some think he is innocent because he've not confessed a word.'

Mr Erle, the defence counsel, was indeed determined that John Russell should not hang and immediately the trial was over he left Taunton for Chard to carry out further enquiries and the examination of witnesses.

Meanwhile John Russell was conveyed to Ilchester Gaol where at ten o'clock on the morning of Saturday 10 April, he would mount the gallows and be hanged by the neck until he was dead.

On the Good Friday night, the condemned man slept well, perhaps dreaming of a man who hung on a Cross in a far away country a long long time ago, and when he rose at seven o'clock on the morning of his execution, he told his gaolers that he was ready to meet his Maker for a crime of which he had no knowledge. It was then John Russell was told that Mr Justice Gaselee, following strong representations from Mr Erle, had stayed the execution until 28 April. It was reported that the news seemed to have little effect upon him.

The stay of execution caused a sensation and the press joined in the general excitement. Report followed report and rumour followed rumour. Mr Erle was in Chard questioning witnesses, three county magistrates were also making enquiries and the prisoner had implicated someone else. It was said that two men were in custody following statements from the prisoner's wife and that three men had been involved in the murder, one had held the young woman's legs, another her arms and the third had cut her throat. There was a suggestion that the unsolved murder of thirteen-year-old Betty Trump six years before at nearby Buckland St Mary, bore a similarity to the murder of Joan Turner.

Such were some of the rumours and stories circulating in the Chard area, and even the prestigious *Times* joined in, its edition of Saturday 10 April recording that 'every hour seems to increase the anxiety felt here, and which it is impossible for any person to describe.'

Meanwhile, William Erle's enquiries were uncovering some disturbing facts involving malicious gossip taken as truth, half-truths, intimidaton, interference, ridicule and the imprisonment of two possible defence witnesses during the trial. Eventually, on 27 April, William Erle presented a Petition to the Right Honourable Robert Peel, the Home Secretary, seeking the King's mercy for John Russell.

The Petition addressed in detail the following ten heads of evidence:

1 The motive for the crime
2 The declarations of the prisoner before the murder
3 The conduct of the prisoner at the time of the murder
4 His mention of it before he could have heard of it from others
5 The marks on his face
6 The indications from his clothes which showed no bloodstains
7 The noise of voices and pumping heard from his house and the lights seen on the night of the murder and the bloody water found in the pump the morning after
8 The account given of the prisoner's actions on that night which were shown to be false
9 The declarations made after the murder
10 The marks of blood found in the house

William Erle concluded by sincerely apologizing for the length of the Petition but stated that if he had not been deeply concerned that the prosecution was mistaken, he would not have offered it in such detail.

The Home Secretary immediately transmitted the Petition to Mr Justice Gaselee, who, following his decision to grant a stay of execution, had requested three Somerset magistrates, Mr Hobhouse, Mr Phelips and Mr Coombe, to go to Chard and carry out an investigation into various matters which had arisen subsequent to the trial.

After considering the Petition and the magistrates' report which tended to confirm Mr Erle's concerns, Mr Justice Gaselee, on 10 May, wrote to the Home Secretary stating that it appeared to him to 'be advisable that the convict should not be executed but should be transported for Life.' The letter is set out in the Appendix. On the cover sheet of the judge's letter, the Right Honourable Robert Peel has written, 'John Russell to be transported for Life, May 11 1830'.

Early in June 1830, John Russell was taken from Ilchester Gaol and delivered to the Devonport prison hulk *Captivity* to await transportation to Australia for the rest of his natural life.

Arthur Hull noted in his diary under 'Remarks' that 'J Russel is transported for life tho' not confessed a word' and the *Western Flying Post* reported indignantly that the respites of the convict had cost the County of Somerset £444.

There is a story in the Russell family told to me by a distant relative, Mrs Holland, that one night, many years after the events of 1830, John Russell's aged mother heard a noise at her door and going out to investigate, saw a tramp. There was something familiar about the man and suddenly the old lady recognised him as her son John. He would not stay because he said he felt so ashamed of what had happened but he said that he had just wanted to see her once before he died and with that he disappeared for ever.

Did John Russell murder Joan Turner on that dark November night nearly 170 years ago? We shall never know.

'THAT FISHER'S MAD!'

Joel Fisher of the 7th Hussars was said to have been a fine soldier. The years of campaigning with the cavalry of the Duke of Wellington against the French in Spain had hardened and steadied him but he needed all his courage on 18 June 1815 as his regiment faced the Grand Army of Napoleon across the Belgian fields in the battle which would go down in history as Waterloo. Twenty-nine years later, the Hussar would show the same courage and steadiness in the face of certain death on the scaffold outside the County Gaol in Taunton.

In the summer of 1844, Weston-super-Mare was described as 'a quiet pretty little sea-bathing place a few miles from Bridgwater', and the landlord of the Devonshire Inn in the High Street was the Waterloo veteran, fifty-two-year-old Joel Fisher. Fisher had been born in the nearby village of Wick St Lawrence, the son of a farm labourer, and for some of his early years he had worked for Joseph Hewlett, a local farmer. The young Fisher then entered service with a Weston surgeon, Mr Bisdee, but after some twelve months in this employment he left in 1811 to enlist in the 7th Hussars. Then followed three years of campaigning with the regiment in Spain and subsequently Joel Fisher's last engagement in the Battle at Waterloo.

For the next nineteen years he served with honour with the 7th and when the colonel of the regiment retired in 1834, Fisher accompanied his commanding officer as his servant. During the nine months he lived with the Colonel, he married his fellow servant and the couple left to set up home in Weston-super-Mare where Fisher was re-engaged by his former master, Mr Bisdee. The Fishers lived contentedly with Mr Bisdee and three children were born, but tragedy struck four years later when Mrs Fisher died, followed soon after by the death of one of their children.

Joel Fisher now made the decision which would eventually lead him to the scaffold; he left Mr Bisdee and married Mary Hyatt, a widow four years his senior with two adult children.

From the first the marriage was in trouble due to Mary's violent temper and the interference of her son and daughter. After a few months the couple, who were now living in Backwell, quarrelled and parted. However, several weeks later, Mary Fisher persuaded her husband to take her back and promised to behave in future. During the following twelve months the Fishers lived in Nailsea and Congresbury but the quarrels soon began again with Mary's daughter, who was now living with the family, taking an active role on her mother's side.

In 1841, Joel Fisher, who had left the army with the small fortune of £300, bought the Devonshire Inn in Weston-super-Mare but the quarrelling continued and the disputes became more frequent. Mary Fisher left her husband on several occasions but, on her promising to behave, the long-suffering husband took her back. Then, in the summer of 1843 the turbulent woman packed up again but this time left taking £20 of her husband's cash and a quantity of linen.

The furious Fisher tracked her down to Bath where he found that the cash had been banked and although Mary had hidden the cheque she finally admitted that it was concealed in her stays and so the cash was recovered. However she refused to return and back home in Weston-super-Mare, Joel Fisher advertised that no one should trust her as his wife and that he would not be responsible for her acts.

After three weeks absence, Mary Fisher began to bombard her husband with messages promising that if he would take her back she would control her temper and never leave him again. Once again Fisher took her back but almost immediately the quarrelling was renewed with even greater intensity!

By the spring of 1844 Joel Fisher, the steadfast old Hussar, was at breaking point. Although he was a reasonably good publican, he could neither read nor write and was dependent upon his wife for the management of his accounts and perhaps this explains why he kept taking her back. The periods of absence and the constant rows were placing an overwhelming burden upon the man as he struggled to keep the business going and at the same time look after his two young sons. Joel Fisher finally broke just after five o'clock in the morning of Tuesday 4 June 1844, when he battered Mary Fisher's head with an iron bar, cut her throat to the backbone, and surrendered to the police.

Weston-super-Mare, the 'quiet pretty little sea bathing place' was thrown into a 'state of awful excitement' by the murder and great was the interest when Joel Fisher stood before Mr Justice Pattison at the Summer Assizes in Wells on Monday 12 August 1844 charged with the 'Wilful Murder of Mary Fisher'.

The case for the prosecution was opened by Mr Stone who outlined the events of 3 and 4 June and called his first witness, the Fishers' servant, Ann Evans. Ann Evans said that she had been with the family for a fortnight prior to the fatal day and during this short time she had witnessed many quarrels and disputes between the Fishers. On one occasion she had been concerned to see her master walking about the inn muttering to himself.

The servant went on to say that at about five o'clock on the afternoon of 3 June, Joel Fisher had returned to the inn after completing some business and was told by his wife that Peter Baker, one of his two lodgers, had left after a row with her and she hoped the other, William Upsall, would follow. Ann Evans then told how at nine o'clock that evening she had taken a lighted candle into the bar which Mrs Fisher blew out and, when she brought in a second, her mistress had blown this one out as well. Joel Fisher ordered another candle to be brought in but his wife retorted that if one was lit the accounts would come out and so saying she picked up the slate and rubbed out all the details of the day's takings. At this the landlord had shouted at his wife that he 'would give it to her by and by; she was asking for it!'

Ann Evans continued with her evidence by describing how she and her mistress had lit candles at about ten o'clock and then both gone upstairs to their bedrooms. The servant went into her room, which she shared with Joel Fisher's two young sons, but she had not been there long when Mrs Fisher came in bringing her a glass of wine and saying she would sleep with Ann. Hearing her husband coming up the stairs she told the servant to lock the bedroom door shouting, 'Oh! that rascal. I'll never sleep with him again!' The couple began to shout at each other through the door and Fisher began to pound on it exclaiming that he was determined to kill his wife that night rather than wait until the next morning. Mrs Fisher then tried to jump out of the window but Ann Evans held her back and calmed her down. However the quarrelling and door banging soon recommenced and continued off and on through the night until everything went quiet at about one o'clock the next morning when Ann Evans finally fell asleep.

She was suddenly woken by a noise and, sitting up, the servant was surprised and then horrified to see her master standing at the foot of the bed holding an iron bar. Shouting, 'Damn your eyes, I'll do for you now!' Ann saw him lunge forward and strike his wife's head several times with the bar and then rush out of the room. The terrified servant scrambled out of the bed but before she could fully recover her senses, Fisher came storming back into the room, leapt onto the bed and standing on his wife's chest, cut her throat with a carving knife. Ann Evans then told how her master had turned to her and calmly said that he had committed no sin but had removed a sinner from the world; she was not to be afraid because he would not hurt her or run away. Fisher then left the bedroom calling for the lodger, William Upsall, while his two boys in a state of terror ran down the stairs to the bar.

The lodger, William Upsall, now entered the witness box and stated that he had gone to bed at ten o'clock on the evening of 3 June. He had heard the Fishers quarrelling on the landing and Mary Fisher shouting that she would never sleep with the old rascal again for as long as she had breath to draw. The quarrelling and the sound of Joel Fisher stomping about the inn had kept the apprehensive lodger awake until well into the early hours and day was breaking when he finally dropped off to sleep. Upsall, however, was soon to be rudely awakened by shouts and screams and, as he clambered out of bed, Joel Fisher burst into his room waving a bloody long-bladed carving knife and crying, 'William, I've done it!'. Horrified at the sight of the bloodstained knife Upsall exclaimed, 'For God's sake you've not killed your children have you?' 'No, but I've killed her!' was the exultant reply.. 'Go and fetch a policeman and give me in charge!'

William Upsall then told the jury how he had tried to calm the landlord and suggested that a doctor should be called but Fisher insisted that his wife was dead and he should fetch a policeman as 'I will be hung for it.' The lodger stated that he had then gone and called on the local surgeon, Mr Bernard, and after telling him what had happened he had hurried on to the local police station.

Constable Robert Hill followed William Upsall into the witness box and testified that the lodger had arrived at the police station between five and six o'clock in the morning of 4 June. He had accompanied Upsall to the Devonshire Inn where they met Mr Bernard who had arrived shortly before. Constable Hill tried the door but found it to be fastened and so had knocked loudly, demanding entrance. Joel Fisher then opened the door and the constable ordered him to stand back as he was coming in. The landlord told the officer there was no need to be afraid as he would not run away and, turning round, he went up the stairs followed by the policeman and the surgeon. Seeing the blood-stained room, and the still figure lying on the bed, Constable Hill immediately arrested Joel Fisher and took him back to the police station. He then returned to the inn to carry out further investigations. The constable stated that he had found the iron bar in an adjoining room and also had taken charge of the bloodstained carving knife.

The last witness for the prosecution was Mr Charles Bernard, the surgeon, who stated that he knew the prisoner and had attended the deceased some months before. He told how he had been called out by Upsall, the lodger, and had gone to the inn only to find the door fastened and one of Fisher's boys standing outside. In answer to his knocking, the surgeon heard the bolt withdrawn but when the door opened, Fisher had looked out and seeing his son had taken him in saying, 'Come in my son; it was for you I did it.' However, before Mr Bernard could follow, the prisoner slammed the door shut and bolted it shouting that he would not let anyone in until the police came. Shortly after Constable Hill and Upsall had arrived and Fisher had let them in. On entering the bedroom, the surgeon noted that blood was splashed on the ceiling and on one of the walls and a woman was lying on the bed. He examined the body, which he recognised as that of Mrs Fisher, and found her to be quite dead. There was a wound in her throat about five inches long and which had divided the carotid artery. The windpipe and gullet were cut through and the bones of the spine had been laid bare. Mr Bernard had also observed three wounds on the dead woman's head but he did not believe they were the cause of her death. Fisher had been present when he had begun his examination of the body and he recalled the prisoner muttering, 'I've done it; I've done it; it's no use; I've done it; I knew I should do it; and I know I should be hung for it. If she had spoken a word to me it might have been prevented. I asked her to speak but she would not.' The surgeon testified that the prisoner had said that he had struck his wife three times with the iron bar but, seeing that she was still breathing, he had fetched the knife and cut her throat because he though he had better finish it.

In conclusion Mr Bernard confirmed that the gaping wound in Mary Fisher's throat had caused her death.

The prosecution's case was now complete and Mr Cockburn, Joel Fisher's counsel, rose and addressed the jury. He said that he would not deny that the prisoner had committed the awful act, but he believed there were features in the case which might lead the jury to consider that the offence of 'Wilful Murder' had not been proven and was capable of being reduced to 'Manslaughter'. It appeared that the deceased was a woman of a most violent and aggravating temper and it was impossible to have listened to the details of the case without being convinced that she was capable of extreme violence of temper and conduct. Mr Cockburn suggested that the jury might consider whether her conduct had led to this tragic end and something had taken place between the husband and wife immediately before her death when no witnesses were present. Counsel reminded the jury that all the time Ann Evans had been awake, her mistress had been with her behind the locked bedroom door. No evidence had been produced which indicated that the door had been broken open so how had the prisoner entered the locked bedroom? Could the deceased have left the room when the servant slept, a personal conflict had then taken place and the prisoner had followed his wife back into the room and killed her?

Mr Cockburn then suggested that the prisoner's actions which followed the crime were not those of a sane man. The prisoner had not harmed the one witness who had seen everything and indeed, it seemed that he had wished her to be a witness! Fisher had then gone to tell the lodger what he had done and asked him to fetch the police. He had also told the surgeon to wait outside until the police arrived and yet he had taken his son back in saying, 'Come in my son. I have done it for you.' What had the fearful act to do with the child and was there the vestige of sanity or reason in the prisoner's conduct? No, it showed that this was incoherent raving; all Fisher's actions after the dreadful deed pointed to madness. Mr Cockburn then said that he would call two witnesses who would speak to the state of the prisoner's mind.

Joseph Hewlett was the first defence witness. He said that he was a farmer living near Weston-super-Mare and had done so for some forty years. Joel Fisher had lived with the family for a while as a farm servant about thirty-six years before. He had always thought that there was something unusual about the prisoner because he had 'a deplorable look about him.' On 25 May last, the witness had been in the Devonshire Inn and had given tenpence for five pints of ale. The prisoner had only taken eightpence but, when Hewlett had pointed out the error, Fisher had flown into a rage and threatened him with a large carving knife. Although there were other customers in the bar, Joseph Hewlett stated that he had been very frightened and had left as quickly as possible for he was in fear of his life. He was sure, however, that the prisoner did not know what he was doing.

The second witness was James Bailey Smith who stated that he was an exciseman and had known Joel Fisher for three years. He had noticed a strangeness in the prisoner's manner during the time he had carried out his regular excise surveys of the inn and on a number of occasions he had remarked, 'That Fisher's mad.'

The judge, Mr Justice Pattison, now began his summing up. He said that the jury must consider whether Mary Fisher had died from the wound, whether the prisoner had inflicted it and then the defence put forward. With regard to the alleged insanity of the prisoner, Mr Justice Pattison explained to the jury that every man must be taken to be sane until the contrary was proved and every man must be taken to know the law of the land. If a man did not know what was wrong he must be considered to be insane, but if he was aware that at the time he committed the act it was wrong, and the act was against the law, then he was responsible for his actions.

After a short retirement the jury returned a verdict of 'Guilty to Wilful Murder'. When asked to say why the judgment to die should not be passed on him, Joel Fisher stated that nothing had been said which ought not to have been; his wife was his complete enemy instead of his friend and he thought that he had better be hung than live with such a wicked woman. He concluded that he was well aware of what he had done and he hoped that the Lord would have mercy on him as a sinner.

Mr Justice Pattison then put on the black cap and pronounced the sentence of death on Joel Fisher. The judge stated that he was sorry to hear the remarks made by the prisoner because it showed a fearful state of mind. He believed that the jury had come to the correct decision and if the deceased was as wicked as stated by the prisoner, he had sent her out of this world without the opportunity to repent and make her peace with God. Mr Justice Pattison earnestly entreated the prisoner to come to a better state of mind in the short time left for there was no hope of mercy being extended to him on this earth. Joel Fisher was then removed from the dock and seemed to be unmoved by the dreadful sentence just passed upon him.

Whilst he was waiting to be taken from Wells to the County Gaol in Taunton, Fisher was allowed to see his sons for the last time. It was reported that the parting was agonizing and, as he gave his treasured Waterloo Medal to his eldest son, Joel Fisher was said to have exclaimed, 'Oh John! Would that I had died at Waterloo. You would never have been born to the disgrace and I should never have committed this dreadful crime.'

A small crowd of about 200 people watched the condemned man leave the court house at Wells for his last journey to the County Gaol and to his execution which would take place on Wednesday 4 September.

Joel Fisher spent his last days in constant prayer and in long discussions with the prison chaplain. He was confined in a light and well-ventilated cell with a small yard for his exercise and an officer was in constant attendance, a contrast with the old system under which the prisoner was fettered and kept in a dark dungeon. There were reports that the Governor had received several requests from people afflicted with rheumatism and the 'King's Evil' (scrofula, or tuberculosis of the lymph glands of the neck) for permission for the dead hand of Joel Fisher to be rubbed over the affected parts, as they believed this would cure them. The local newspapers expressed surprise that such gross superstitions still existed in the year 1844.

On the Monday evening before his execution Joel Fisher was visited by his brother and an old comrade who had served with him for twenty years in the 7th Hussars and who had travelled over a 100 miles to Taunton to see his friend for the last time.

During the night which followed Fisher slept well and remained calm and quiet throughout the long Tuesday. At ten o'clock on the last night the chaplain visited the condemned man and gave him a letter from Thomas Hyatt, his late wife's son, in which he forgave his step-father and which was said to have helped very considerably to quieten the state of his mind.

Joel Fisher rose early on his last morning, ate a light breakfast and then prayed until the chaplain joined him at seven o'clock. At ten o'clock Divine Service commenced, prayers were read and the Sacrament administered.

The procession to the scaffold was then assembled and, accompanied by the chaplain, prison officials and several of his Waterloo companions, Joel Fisher walked firmly into the view of the 3000 spectators crowded in front of the gaol to watch his last moments. With his features firm and without a tremble, Joel Fisher stood steady on the scaffold as the rope was secured and the cap placed over his head. His signal to the hangman was the conclusion of the Lord's Prayer and as the bolts were drawn he called out, 'Oh God pardon my sins and receive my soul!' The old Hussar died instantly.

THE WITHYPOOL POISONER

After only 12 months of marriage, Abraham and Mary Reed were no longer on the best of terms. So when neighbour, Mrs Ann Quick, heard the row from the other side of the thin wall which separated the two households in the remote Exmoor village of Withypool, she took little notice. The sound of of breaking crockery indicated a more than average row but what could you expect from the Reeds and their constant bickering.

Ann Quick later recalled that things went quiet for about half an hour but then she heard Abraham Reed crying out that his wife was ill and could she come and help. Responding to the call, Mrs Quick found her neighbour writhing in what seemed like a fit and being supported in a chair by her husband. The spasms finally ceased and Mary Reed asked for a drink of tea saying that she was feeling a little better.

Later that afternoon Ann Quick heard Abraham Reed calling again that his wife was ill and hastening next door was shocked to see her neighbour being violently sick and screaming that she had been poisoned by arsenic.

At seven o'clock on the evening of Monday 6 July 1829, Mary Reed, aged thirty, died and Abraham Reed began his journey into the Valley of the Shadow of Death.

The trial of Abraham Reed for the 'Wilful Murder of his wife Mary by the administration of arsenic' began at the Somerset Lammas Assizes in Bridgwater on the morning of Friday 27 August 1829. Described as a mild looking man of thirty years of age, the prisoner stood at the bar before Lord Chief Justice Tindall and listened impassively as Mr Erle opened the case for the prosecution. The learned counsel explained to the jury that one class of evidence put forward as proof in a trial for murder by poison and accepted as an undisputable fact was finding poison when the contents of the stomach were subjected to medical tests. On this occasion, however, such proof could not be shown but two medical gentlemen would come before the jury and provide evidence that poison could be taken into the stomach and, although vomited out, could cause sufficient inflammation to result in death.

Mr Erle went on to tell the jury how the prisoner Reed had entered a benefit society at North Molton and, after two years membership, became entitled to receive £6. 5s. 6d. on the death of his wife. Counsel stated that shortly after the prisoner had become so entitled, his wife had eaten some cream for her breakfast and after being taken violently ill, had died some twenty two hours later. He would prove that the prisoner had broken the cup which contained the cream and thrown the pieces into a mud pond in the front yard of his home where the neighbour's pigs and the prisoner's fowls rummaged for scraps. During the days following the death of Mary Reed, one of the pigs had died after violent vomiting and purging and so had three of the fowls.

In concluding his opening statement, Mr Erle said that it would be for the jury to decide whether the prisoner, Reed, had descended into the lowest state of mental depravity and murdered his wife for the trifling sum of money to be paid on her death. After hearing the testimony of the witnesses, counsel believed there would be no shadow of doubt in their minds as to the motive of the prisoner who stood before them.

The first witness was Mrs Catherine Burgess who stated that, with her husband, she kept a shop in the village of North Molton about five miles from Withypool. Early in the morning of Monday 29 June a man whom she now recognised as the prisoner, had called at the shop and asked if they sold mercury or arsenic. When Mrs Burgess said no, the prisoner asked if they sold Spanish Flies? The witness told him that no poisons of any sort were sold in their shop and when he asked where he might buy some she directed him to Mr Westcott, the village tailor, who also sold groceries and drugs.

Henry Westcott now took the stand and said that the prisoner had come to his father's shop early the same morning asking if could buy some arsenic. As he was not acquainted with arsenic the witness went upstairs to rouse his father who was still in bed and told him of the prisoner's request. When his father came down he heard the prisoner ask for arsenic and some was obtained from the shop, wrapped in paper with the word 'Poison' written on the packet and handed to Abraham Reed. The witness had never seen the prisoner before.

Mr Westcott, senior, recognised Abraham Reed as the man who had told him that he wanted to kill rats and to whom he had sold three ounces of arsenic for sixpence. After writing 'Poison' on the packet he had warned the prisoner to take care of it. Mr Westcott stated that Abraham Reed had asked for the poison quite publicly but the witness was admonished by the Lord Chief Justice for selling arsenic to a stranger and instructed never to do so again. The witness confirmed that a sample of arsenic from the same jar had been given to the prosecuting counsel's clerk.

Robert Stoneman, a member of the benefit club, recalled that early in the morning of 29 June he had met the prisoner leaving North Molton and during their conversation Abraham Reed had wondered how much he would get from the club if his wife died. The witness thought that it would be between six and seven pounds.

Richard Hole, who farmed at Knighton, near Withypool, stated that the prisoner had worked for him from time to time and on the morning of 7 July had borrowed a horse to ride to North Molton to collect the club money for his wife's funeral. Farmer Hole was followed by his mother, Joan, who testified that as Abraham Reed was leaving work on Saturday 4 July he had asked if she could spare some cream and on the following morning had called for it between nine and ten o'clock. Mrs Hole had poured the thick cream into the clean cup which the prisoner had brought and she was certain that he did not eat any before he left. The witness went on to say that her family of ten had eaten the remainder of the cream at dinner and tea and had not been ill.

The next witness was Mrs Ann Quick who stated that she was the wife of James Quick and that Abraham and Mary Reed had resided next door since the previous March. The two families lived in the same cottage with a wall dividing them and in a corner of the shared front yard was a mud pond used by her husband's pigs and the prisoner's fowls.

During the evening of Saturday 4 July the witness had seen Mary Reed who appeared to be in good health. She told the jury that the Reeds had not lived happily together for some time and on the following morning at about ten o'clock Ann Quick had heard the couple quarrelling and the sound of breaking crockery. It had then gone quiet but about half an hour later Abraham Reed had called through the wall that his wife was ill. Going next door, the witness had found Mary in a chair having what seemed like a fit and being supported by her husband. After about ten minutes the convulsions ceased and the sick woman asked for a kettle to be boiled for a cup of tea. Abraham Reed obtained some water and after drinking some tea Mary seemed better.

Ann Quick returned to her kitchen and at about five o'clock that afternoon she saw the Reeds walking around the front yard. However, shortly after the prisoner called again for his neighbour and this time the witness was alarmed at what she saw. Mary Reed was writhing in agony and was being violently sick. On seeing her neighbour, Mary cried out several times that she had been poisoned and beseeched her to send for a doctor as she thought she was about to die. Ann tried to comfort Mary and asked why she thought she had been poisoned. 'I ate some cream my husband brought down from Knighton and they had put arsenic in it,' she had gasped in reply. The witness recalled that she had dismissed this suggestion and asked to see the cream but Mary Reed told her that the portion she had not eaten had been tipped into the mud pond by her husband who had broken the cup and thrown it away.

Ann asked Abraham Reed if he had eaten any of the cream and he had said that he had some at Knighton farm. She should not take any notice of his wife because she was always claiming that things he brought into the house were dirty or poisoned and he had a good mind never to bring anything back again.

Becoming increasingly concerned at Mary Reed's condition, the witness suggested to Abraham that he should go for a doctor but Mary became agitated, crying that if he did so he would never come back; a doctor was not called.

Ann Quick then recalled that Mary Reed continued to be violently sick and complained of severe stomach pains throughout the Sunday evening but being unable to give any more help she had returned home. Going next door the following morning the witness was distressed to find that Mary in bed suffering extreme pain in her stomach and pleading for the parish clergyman, the Reverend Mr Boyce, to come and bleed her. Ann stated that she had called on the reverend gentleman but on her return she was met by a distraught Abraham Reed weeping and exclaiming that his wife had died.

Ann then recounted how on Monday 6 July her two pigs which lived in the front yard had been perfectly healthy but on the following afternoon, when she had taken them their food, one would not eat and by evening was dead after manifesting similar symptoms to Mary Reed. One of the prisoner's fowls had died on Monday, the second on Tuesday and the third on Wednesday. The pigs and the fowls had access to the mud pond.

The village undertaker and carpenter, John Thorne, now took the stand and recounted his conversation with the prisoner when Mary Reed's body was being placed in her coffin. Thorne had mentioned the village gossip about Mary's death and stated that the women who had laid her out were suggesting that Mr Collyns, the Dulverton surgeon, should examine the body. He went on to say that he had strongly advised Abraham Reed to go to the surgeon so that the rumours could be put to rest. Although the prisoner had been reluctant to go he had finally borrowed a horse from Farmer Hole and set out for Dulverton. John Thorne recalled that when the prisoner returned later that evening he told the undertaker that Mr Collyns would come to examine his wife's corpse on the morrow. Abraham Reed had then wondered how he could prevent the surgeon from opening the body for he would never allow this to be done. He said that during her lifetime his wife had expressed a strong objection to such an examination and had proclaimed that the person who opened her would have no peace on earth for she would haunt him for as long as he lived.

The undertaker said that he had never known anyone being opened before Mary Reed and explained that the village people had a strong dislike of the bodies of their relations and friends being treated in this manner. Mr John Lockyer Passmore, Mr Erle's clerk, now produced the sample of arsenic he had obtained from Mr Westcott and which had been handed to Mr Collyns, the surgeon.

Mr Charles Palk Collyns, surgeon of Dulverton, followed Passmore into the witness box. He stated that Abraham Reed had called at his house at about five o'clock on the afternoon of Tuesday 7 July, and asked him to go to Withypool to see his wife, who had died the day before, because his neighbours claimed that she had been poisoned. The prisoner had gone on to describe the symptoms and the manner in which the woman had died. Mr Collyns had ridden to Withypool the following day and on opening the body he had found the stomach and intestines to be very inflamed. He removed these organs and sealed them in a bottle for further examination but before he left the prisoner's house he was told by the neighbours of the death of the Quick's pig. On opening the animal the surgeon found the stomach and intestines to be highly inflamed and he removed the organs and sealed them in a second bottle for later examination

Mr Collyns then explained the tests he had made for arsenic or other corrosive sublimates but stated that he could find no evidence of any poison in the human or animal organs. However, the severe inflammation could not be explained by natural disease. Wishing to seek the opinion of a more experienced colleague, Mr Collyns travelled to Taunton to consult Mr Hugh Standert, surgeon, of East Reach.

The organs of Mary Reed and the unfortunate pig were subjected by both surgeons to several chemical tests and examined microscopically but there were no signs of arsenic or any other poison.

Returning to Withypool without proof of arsenical poisoning, Mr Collyns tried one more series of chemical tests but these also proved negative. Abraham Reed, if he ever felt the cold hand of death lift from his shoulders, must have felt the pressure ease at this moment. The medical evidence had clearly shown no signs of poison in his wife's body and, without such proof, how could anyone find him guilty of murder? The cold hand, however, resumed its grip when Mr Collyns stated that a large amount of arsenic could have been taken on the Sunday morning and although vomited by Mary Reed, could have remained in the stomach long enough to cause inflammation sufficient to cause death. The same could equally apply to the pig which had also voided the contents of its stomach. In the surgeon's opinion the symptoms described by the witnesses and the prisoner could have been caused by arsenical poisoning. Once again he emphasised that the condition of the deceased woman's organs could not be accounted for by natural causes.

Mr Collyns stated that on Saturday 11 July he had visited the prisoner who was in bed in a neighbour's house. Abraham Reed had complained of being unwell but appeared to be suffering more in mind than in body. He had beseeched the surgeon to befriend him and had offered him money to do so. Mr Collyns had promised to do what he could consistent with his duty, but of course he had declined to accept the money. He asked Abraham Reed if he had used poison for any purpose, but this the prisoner denied, saying that he would not know poison if he saw it. However he had then gone on to say that he had seen his mother-in-law mixing meal in a pan to which poison had been added for baiting rats. The prisoner said his wife knew that poison was at her mother's home and occasionally she got cream there. Mr Standert, the Taunton surgeon, followed his medical colleague and supported his conclusions.

The prosecution now brought to the stand two witnesses to prove the prisoner's intent to dispose of his wife. Ann Colmer recalled a conversation about three weeks before Mary died when Abraham Reed had said that he intended to go to the fair at the nearby village of Winsford on Monday 6 July if his wife died before then. Ann Colmer, somewhat surprised at this statement, enquired why he thought his wife would die because the witness had seen her in good health during the previous day. 'Not a fortnight longer! Mark my words', was Reed's reply. Ann Colmer went on to say that this conversation had been overheard by her friend, Miss Hole.

Next to be examined was William Chamberlain who said that at about the time mentioned by Ann Colmer, Abraham Reed had told him that he wanted some mercury or arsenic to poison rats and enquired if there was a druggist's shop in Porlock.

Last to give evidence was the coroner, Mr R.P. Caines, who had held the inquest on the body of Mary Reed on 12 July. During his examination, the prisoner had sworn that he had only been in two houses in North Molton on 29 June, namely the inn and Kingdon's where he had paid the balance of his subscription to the benefit club.

The case for the Crown was now complete but no defence was put forward other than Abraham Reed declaring that he was innocent. The Lord Chief Justice then summed up the evidence in great detail and the jury, after a few minutes consultation, returned a verdict of 'Guilty'. The *Taunton Courier* reported that 'the prisoner did not display any particular feeling of interest till the evidence of the medical men was taken, when he appeared to rouse himself from the apathy that possessed him at other periods of the proceedings. The jury having pronounced their verdict of 'Guilty', the prisoner was called upon to say why judgement of death should not be pronounced against him: a slight convulsion passed over his features for a single moment and he muttered in an indistinct tone, 'The witnesses have sworn falsely'. It seemed, however, as if the senses of the unhappy man were lost in reverie; he appeared in a sort of waking dream and remained, with fixed eyes, leaning upon the bar, till the gaoler seizing him suddenly by the arm when he again started as when first placed in the dock, and hastily retired.'

The sentence of the court was not long delayed and Abraham Reed's appointment with the hangman was fixed for the next Monday, 30 August at Ilchester Gaol. He spent the Friday night following his trial in the gaol at Bridgwater and on the Saturday morning confessed his guilt to the Under Sheriff of Somerset admitting that the marriage had not been happy and he had mixed about one and a half ounces of the arsenic into the cream given to his wife.

Abraham Reed arrived at Ilchester on the Saturday afternoon and attended Sunday service in the chapel when he heard the chaplain preach on the text, 'Thou shalt not kill'. The condemned man was reported to have been much affected by the words. The chaplain remained with the prisoner for most of the remaining hours of his life and on the Monday morning he administered the Sacrament

At half past eleven Abraham Reed was pinioned and slowly the procession of the condemned advanced to the scaffold outside the gaol and the waiting crowd. After praying for a short while, the signal was given, the platform dropped and Abraham Reed passed through the Valley of the Shadow of Death. It was said that he suffered much in those last few minutes but not so much as Mary, just under two months before.

THE MALIGNANT SHOOTING
OF JOSEPH DUNFORD

Resentment, hurt pride, real or imagined slights, can form a dangerous cocktail of emotions and when fuelled by alcohol the mixture can be explosive as the events of a May evening in 1835 were to prove.

For over half a century, four generations of the Plumley family had served the Pigotts of Brockley Hall, near Backwell, as game-keepers, and the fourth, twenty-five-year-old John, had been proud to be headkeeper – that is until Joseph Dunford was engaged in the spring of 1834.

At first the estate was divided between the two men but after eight months, the owner, J.H.S. Pigott Esq., appointed Joseph Dunford as head-keeper and John Plumley was demoted to under-keeper. The record is silent on the reasons for the change of status but John Plumley's feelings of resentment and hurt pride must have been compounded by the removal of his authority to carry a gun at all times on the estate; only the head-keeper was allowed this privilege.

Head-keeper Dunford was getting annoyed! Where the devil was John Plumley; he should have been here by now to help under-keeper Charles Coleman and William Blackwood, the gardener, dig out a fox at the edge of a plantation of young trees. It was seven o'clock on the evening of 11 May 1835 and the light would soon be fading.

William Blackwood had met Plumley earlier in the evening just after the under-keeper had shot a fox, but after examining the dead animal, the gardener had left to make his way across the park to rendezvous with Dunford and Coleman. He told the head-keeper that he had seen Plumley but had no idea how long he would take to arrive.

At last the errant under-keeper came strolling through the trees and Charles Coleman shouted a greeting. Plumley had been walking along the opposite side of the paling fence which enclosed the plan-tation, but before he could cross, Coleman asked to see the fox which he had shot. As the under-keeper pulled the dead fox from his pocket, Joseph Dunford remarked that as it was so small there had been no need to shoot it, he could have easily caught the animal.

'Damn you, Dunford!' snarled Plumley, who was exhibiting signs of too much alcohol. 'I'll shoot any vermin I care to!'

'Where have you been to all day?' demanded the head-keeper, ignoring the gibe and controlling his temper.

'Down in the Coomb.'

'You could not have been there, so where have you been? You should have met us long past to dig this fox and you've had drink!' Dunford responded angrily.

'You're a damned liar!' swore Plumley.

At this insult, Joseph Dunford, a big man well over six feet tall, lost his temper and advancing towards Plumley who was still standing on the other side of the fence, roared, 'If you call me a liar I'll knock your head off!'

The months of resentment, hurt and imagined slights finally surfaced and yelling, 'You are a damned liar!' John Plumley raised the gun to his shoulder and squeezed the trigger. Nothing happened, the gun had not been cocked. Plumley, consumed by blind rage, lowered the gun, cocked it, raised it to his shoulder once again and fired. The full contents of the barrel tore a hole two inches square in Joseph Dunford's chest and blew out one of his ribs. The head-keeper died almost immediately but not before crying out, 'Lord have mercy on my wife and family. Plumley thou hast done it at last!'

For a moment, as the smoke drifted away, Charles Coleman and William Blackwood stared in horror at the carnage but then, shouting 'You rascal you'll be hanged for this!' Coleman vaulted the fence and threw himself on Plumley beating him with the stick he was carrying. Coleman then leapt back over the palings and, picking up Dunford's gun, threatened to shoot Plumley but further bloodshed was avoided by the timely intervention of Blackwood who seized the weapon before it could be used.

John Plumley offered no resistance and did not try to escape; the murderous rage had gone.

The inquest into the death of Joseph Dunford was held a few days later and the coroner's jury unanimously returned a verdict of manslaughter against John Plumley who was escorted to Shepton Mallet Gaol to await trial at the forthcoming Assizes.

The trial was held before Judge Baron Gurney at the Somerset Lammas Assizes in Bridgwater of Thursday 13 August 1835. Although the inquest jury had returned a verdict of manslaughter, the Grand Jury had charged John Plumley with 'the Wilful Murder of Joseph Dunford.' In 1835 a prisoner found guilty of murder would invariably be sentenced to death by hanging but manslaughter did not carry a capital conviction; to be found guilty of manslaughter could mean anything from a short prison term to transportation for life but you would not be hanged. The jury that was to try Plumley had two courses open to them; they could find him guilty of murder and if so he would hang or they could find him guilty of manslaughter and almost certainly he would be transported for life because a shooting of this nature would not warrant a prison term. Would the jury accept the verdict of the inquest or that of the Grand Jury?

The trial opened with Mr Bere conducting the prosecution and Mr Rogers and Mr Moody appearing for the prisoner.

The under-keeper, Charles Coleman, was the first witness and he described the events of the evening of 11 May which had resulted in the shooting to death of Joseph Dunford. Cross-examined by Mr Rogers, the witness stated that following the appointment of the deceased as head-keeper, the prisoner was not allowed to carry a gun on the estate. He could not recollect beating Plumley or picking up Dunford's gun and threatening to shoot him. Coleman went on to say that he had never had a quarrel with the prisoner before the shooting.

William Blackwood, the gardener, corroborated the last witness's evidence but added that Coleman had seized Plumley and struck him two or three times. He had shouted at Coleman not to hurt the prisoner and then disarmed the enraged under-keeper, who was behaving like a madman and threatening to shoot Plumley. Cross-examined, the witness thought that Joseph Dunford was going to strike the prisoner when he had threatened to knock his head off. He also recollected Plumley complaining of Dunford being placed over him and had said that the head-keeper was trying to get his place.

Thomas Jenkin, a labourer employed on the estate, recalled a conversation with the prisoner on the evening in question when he had complained about the head-keeper, saying that he would stop Dunford before long. The witness said that the prisoner appeared to be drinking but he could not remember if he had a gun.

Witness John Bush, a Brockley carpenter, remembered the prisoner telling him a few days before the shooting that Joseph Dunford was informing Mr Pigott of everything he could against him to get him out of his 'berth' and everything he did was wrong. The prisoner had gone on to say that he expected some bother when he got home because the deer had knocked down some of the paling fence of the Park plantation and he had not reported it to the Steward. Dunford was always watching his premises and if he caught him there 'he must charge his rifle for him.' The witness said that

Plumley was sober when he made these remarks. John Parsons testified that on the previous Lady Day, the prisoner had told him that Joseph Dunford was always complaining about the deer and said he would shoot him or something to that effect.

Mr J.H.S. Pigott, of Brockley Hall, entered the witness box and stated that Plumley had been his head-keeper but when Dunford came into his service he had divided the estate between them for eight months. He had then appointed Dunford as head-keeper and Plumley had been forbidden to carry a gun. Cross-examined, Mr Pigott stated that the prisoner's father, grandfather and great-grandfather had been in the employ of his family. He went on to say that he had always considered the prisoner to be a very humane man.

John Taylor, servant to Mr Pigott, testified that on the Saturday before Dunford's death, the prisoner had come to Brockley Hall asking for his gun to shoot rabbits and, with his master's consent, he had given it to him. Cross-examined, the witness said that he had never heard John Plumley quarrel with anyone.

The last witness was surgeon James Hurd, who had been called to the dead man's cottage and examined the body. Dunford was quite dead from a gunshot wound in the left breast.

The case for the prosecution having closed John Plumley put in a written defence. He stated that he believed Dunford had been going to attack him and had put up his gun to defend himself but knew nothing more until he saw him fall dead. The prisoner had no ill will towards the dead man and the shooting had not been a deliberate act.

Several people were now called and gave the prisoner a 'most excellent character.' The judge, Baron Gurney, then proceeded to sum up the case for the jury. He stated that they were charged with an indictment found by the Grand Jury, which imputed to the prisoner the crime of murder and with the presentment of the coroner's inquest which imputed to him manslaughter. It was their duty to attend to all the evidence which had been given, and to decide whether the prisoner was guilty or not guilty of either of these crimes. The only question was whether, from the evidence they had heard, the offence was murder or manslaughter, because beyond all doubt, the deceased had met with his death by the hand of the prisoner and the act was not attended with any circumstance which could possibly reduce it below one of these offences.

Before they considered their verdict Baron Gurney advised the jury of the importance of this matter to the public as well as to the prisoner and, laying aside false pity, they should take this into mind and form their own judgement upon the evidence. The jury then retired and after half an hour returned and delivered a verdict of 'Guilty of Murder' at which the prisoner lowered his head and, with his eyes on the floor of the dock, remained in this position until he was removed at the end of the proceedings.

The court was called to order and Baron Gurney put on the black cap to indicate the sentence he was about to deliver. In a voice trembling with emotion the judge addressed the prisoner at the bar: 'John Plumley, after a patient and deliberate trial and a full consideration of all the evidence, the jury found it to be their painful duty to pronounce a verdict of guilty and, in truth, the evidence left them no choice upon the subject, although they have with every possible attention both to justice and humanity bestowed upon it the fullest consideration they could give. You are a melancholy instance of the danger resulting from the indulgence of the passion of hatred, whether the injuries were real or supposed, and it is but too apparent that your feelings towards the unfortunate deceased were of a malignant kind. You availed yourself of that which no good man would have conceived to be a provocation to take away the life of a fellow servant, you sent him in a moment to answer at the Bar of God with hardly an instant to petition for mercy. He who wilfully sheds man's blood by man must his blood be shed. The time which the law allows is very short, but it is long compared with that which you allowed to the unfortunate sufferer from your violence. Apply by fervent prayer to the God of Mercy for that mercy in the next world which cannot be extended to you in this. I have only to perform the painful but necessary duty of passing upon you the sentence of the law which is, that you be taken to the place from whence you came, and that, on Saturday morning next, you be taken to a place of execution and hanged by the neck until you are dead, and your body be buried within the precincts of the gaol and may the God of all goodness have mercy on your soul.'

It was reported that as he was taken from the dock the prisoner seemed to be 'in a state of great agony.'

As a gesture of mercy, Baron Gurney respited the execution from Saturday to Monday. During the evening following his trial, John Plumley was visited for the last time by his mother and young wife and child. It is not difficult to imagine, even from this distance in time, the emotions of that terrible parting. The condemned man was conveyed on Friday morning to the gaol at Ilchester and on Sunday he bade last farewells to his three sisters and two brothers.

At half past nine on Monday morning, 17 August, the Under Sheriff arrived at the gaol to prepare for the execution, prayers were read and the sacrament taken in the chapel. The prisoner was pinioned and, at 11.15 am, the procession of the condemned advanced slowly to the scaffold. The drop fell at twenty-five minutes to noon and John Plumley died with little suffering before a small crowd.

A JEALOUSY AS CRUEL
AS THE GRAVE

Joseph Wedlake was in love, but his love was not open and honest, but secret, possessive and as cruel as the grave; that was how it was described when he was on trial for his life at the Somerset Spring Assizes in April, 1883.

Farmer Charles Pearce and his wife Mercy were childless but into their home in the hamlet of Ridgehill (or Regil), south of Winford, they had taken their nephew, nine-year-old Joseph Wedlake. Joseph grew up to be a good looking young man and twenty years later, in the winter of 1882, he was his uncle's cowman and well thought of in the small community. However, despite his good looks and thinking himself something of a ladies' man, Joseph could become very jealous of any rival.

Emma Pearce, Mercy's niece, had joined the household when she was eleven and had now grown into a handsome twenty-one-year-old young woman, helping her aunt in the farm dairy. During those early years Joseph had treated Emma like a younger sister but as she developed into womanhood, his feelings had slowly changed – he had fallen in love with her. He had never expressed or shown his love but had worshipped from afar and Emma, unaware of Joseph's passions, had not returned them. How long Joseph's love would have remained burning in secret will never be known and, save for the circumstances which occurred during the closing months of 1882, it might have developed into a mutual love or died in the arms of someone else. However, fate was to deal a different and ultimately fatal hand to Joseph Wedlake.

Emma worshipped at Winford parish church and Joseph would often walk home with her along the narrow road to Ridgehill. In the late autumn of 1882, Alfred Thatcher, a nineteen-year-old farmer's son from the nearby hamlet of Downside, became friendly with Emma and within a short time he was walking her home. Very soon Alfred was courting Emma and after the walk back from the evening service he would occasionally remain at the farm for Sunday supper.

Joseph Wedlake watched the developing romance with dismay and increasing jealousy as the love of his life seemed to be slipping into the arms of another man. When it had been just the two of them living and working together on the farm, Joseph had never felt the need to let Emma know of his love, but now, now it would be too late unless he could do something to prevent the affair from developing further. His mind seethed with jealousy and hatred for the interloper who had invaded his world and stolen his sweetheart. To the outside world however, Joseph was still the same calm, friendly cowman and 'older brother'.

On the Sunday evening before Christmas, Alfred and Emma were chatting at the garden gate at the Pearce farm, when Joseph walked up to the couple and thrusting his lantern close to the young farmer's face exclaimed, 'I've come to see whether you're good looking or no!'

'Don't you think we are?' Alfred jokingly replied.

'There's not much the matter,' mumbled Joseph and walked away.

'Who was he?' enquired the amused Alfred.

'That's my cousin Joseph Wedlake,' replied Emma. 'He's the one I told you lives with us on the farm and helps uncle with the cows.'

Joseph raged at this good looking rival and during the Christmas period a plan began to form in his fevered mind. He would kill Alfred Thatcher as the young farmer walked home after his next visit. The roads around Winford were usually deserted late at night and no one would, or could suspect him of the crime. Why should they? He had no open quarrel with Alfred Thatcher and of course no one would see him do it. How could he kill Alfred Thatcher? This took a little thought but then came the answer. He would use the blunted axe with which he and his uncle stunned the pigs before sticking and bleeding the animals. Joseph was used to wielding the 'pig' axe, and if it could stun a pig it could kill a man.

Alfred Thatcher did not meet Emma again until Sunday 7 January and when the couple arrived back at the farm after their walk from church, they found a friend, Bessie Marshall from Nempnett, chatting to the Pearces in the cosy kitchen. The company broke up at about 10 pm and Alfred and Emma set out with Bessie to walk her back to meet her father at Farmer Weaver's.

Joseph Wedlake had made his plan and now awaited the opportunity. Alfred Thatcher and Emma had arrived at the farm at about 9 pm and Joseph had kept out of sight by working around the outbuildings. The night was cold, foggy and very dark but this would provide all the cover he needed. He watched the three young people leave and saw the glow of the oil lamp in his uncle's bedroom indicating the couple had retired to bed for the night. Joseph went back into the farmhouse, lit a lamp and, making certain that his uncle heard him, walked about the yard and stable as he settled the horses.

He then returned to the house, took off his boots as noisily as possible and climbed the stairs to his room ensuring that they creaked. Joseph took a good mouthful of whisky, slipped the flask into a pocket and crept silently back down the stairs, hauled on his boots and putting on the long working coat he shared with his uncle, slipped out and stole silently across the yard. Having collected the 'pig' axe which he had taken from the cellar and hidden earlier in the day, Joseph hurried after the trio.

Alfred Thatcher was the first to hear the footsteps coming up behind and suggested to Emma and Bessie to keep over to enable the walker to pass. Looking back he could see no one in the darkness but whoever was walking behind made no attempt to overtake them and continued to keep pace for about five minutes; then the footsteps stopped. Suddenly the figure of a man loomed out of the darkness coming towards the trio from the direction of Strode hamlet but did not speak as he passed and was not recognised.

Leaving Bessie Marshall with her father, Alfred and Emma strolled back home arriving at about ten past eleven and went into the warm kitchen where they remained talking.

Joseph had soon caught up with the three young people and kept pace for a short while but broke off as they neared Farmer Weaver's and stood back into a gateway. A figure suddenly appeared coming from their direction and as it came level, Joseph recognised his younger brother Thomas. After greeting his brother, Joseph asked if he had seen anyone on the road and when he said that he had passed three people near Weaver's farm, Joseph exclaimed, ' That was Thatcher, our maid and Bessie Marshall! I'm going to kill Thatcher with the thing we kill the pigs with!'

'Get on with your bother, don't be daft, go home to bed,' Thomas chided.

'No I'm going to kill that Thatcher!' his brother hissed.

Thomas had known for some time that Joseph was very fond of Emma and jealous of Alfred Thatcher but he did not take this outburst seriously as he could smell drink on his brother's breath and he had made threats in the past. No more was said about Thatcher as the two brothers walked back along the road and the conversation turned to the evening Thomas had just spent drinking at Butcombe. Outside Ridgehill Baptist Chapel the brothers parted but as he turned to walk to his father's house, Thomas noticed a bulge at the back of Joseph's long coat as if he was trying to hide something and for a moment he wondered whether Joseph was serious in his threats against Alfred Thatcher.

Joseph Wedlake began to walk back along Ridgehill Street; it would not be long now and Thatcher would say his goodnights and then make his way home to Downside. However, just past the chapel a figure loomed out of the darkness coming from the direction of Winsford. Pulling his hat well down and shrinking into the large coat collars he passed the traveller whom he recognised as Charles Horler hurrying home to Strode. Neither wished each other goodnight and although Horler did not recognise Joseph Wedlake, he recalled later that he noticed the passerby's long coat stuck out at the back as if something was being hidden.

Some 75 yards beyond Farmer King's house and near the cross roads at the end of Ridgehill Street, Joseph stood back in the gloom of the bank and hedge and, sipping his whisky to keep out the cold and bolster his courage, waited for the hated Thatcher.

Mark Cox worked on the night shift at Winford Iron Ore and Redding Works and set out from his home at Ridgehill to walk the $1^1/_2$ miles to the mine at about half past eleven on the Sunday night. For some time he had been nervous about walking alone through Ridgehill in the dark because of a beating and threats he had received from Job Wedlake whom he had accused of shooting some of his pigeons. The walk to work took him past Wedlake's cottage but so far the threats had proved groundless.

Mark eased his flask and food basket on his left shoulder and walked quickly along Ridgehill Street. He passed Farmer King's but just before the cross roads where he would turn off for the Works he glimpsed a sudden movement on his left and a voice said, 'Goodnight.'

Joseph Wedlake heard the footsteps coming towards him and gripped the handle of the axe more firmly. Hatred burned inside him but he was deadly calm. Thatcher was coming. The footsteps came closer and as they came level Joseph stepped forward, 'Goodnight,' he said and swung the axe with all the strength he could muster; in the moment before the blow landed, Joseph realised that this was not Thatcher! The blunt 'pig' axe struck Mark Cox a tremendous blow between his left eye and ear and he fell backwards unconscious. Wedlake watched in horror as the blow landed and the young man went down. The madness, however, was still within him and for a reason he could never understand, he bent over the unconscious form and killed Mark Cox with two more savage blows to his head.

Still clutching the weapon, the murderer hurried back along Ridgehill Street, his mind in a turmoil and wishing to God that he could change the last few minutes.

The sweethearts were cosy in the warm farmhouse kitchen out of the cold and foggy January night when suddenly Alfred heard a sound outside. A stair creaked, then another, then a door creaked up on the landing, then silence. When he mentioned this to Emma, she laughed and said that the old house was always creaking. Alfred later recalled that he thought the noise on the stairs happened at about midnight because he did not leave the farm until well past that hour. The young farmer's walk home to Downside in the small hours of Monday was uneventful and although he passed the body of Mark Cox, he did not see it because the night was so very dark.

John Habberfield, a farm bailiff from Dundry, discovered the body as he made his way home from Ridgehill early on the Monday morning. The Winford policeman, Constable Orman was called and noted that the corpse was lying on the left hand side of the road about 75 yards north of Mr Alfred King's farm. The body, which had already been identified as Mark Cox, lay on its back with the feet pointing towards Winford and the head towards Ridgehill. The left hand was in the trouser pocket and the right hand on the breast. Mark's hat lay underneath his head and was full of blood. His flask and food basket were slung across the left shoulder. Constable Orman also noted that the deceased's clothes were brown and heavily stained with iron ore which blended with the colour of the road.

The report of the finding of the body spread rapidly through the small community and before long villagers, including Joseph and Thomas Wedlake, were coming to inspect the corpse. Thomas noticed nothing unusual in his brother's demeanour but was somewhat surprised when Joseph asked him to say nothing about their meeting the previous evening.

Superintendent John Drewett from Long Ashton police station arrived and took charge of the case. The body of Mark Cox was taken to his home where it was examined by Mr Charles Collins and Mr W. Richardson Edmond, surgeons from Chew Magna. They discovered three massive wounds to the head which the surgeons suggested were delivered in the following sequence. The first blow caused an extensive wound over the left eye-brow extending an inch towards the nose and outwards about four inches towards the ear and underneath there was a depressed fracture of the skull; this blow would have caused immediate unconsciousness. The second would have been delivered when the victim's head was on the ground and was an immense contusion wound over the left ear, with corresponding fractures of the skull and rupturing of blood vessels; this was the blow which had killed Mark Cox. The third had fractured the lower left jaw in two places.

Superintendent Drewett's enquiries in Ridgehill soon turned up Job Wedlake as a prime suspect. His beating of Mark Cox during the previous summer and his many threats were well known. The police had discovered clog prints leading from a field near the murder site through a hedge at the back of the Wedlake cottage and Job was the only member of the household who wore clogs. Despite the family swearing that Job had not left home from early on the Sunday evening until Monday morning, he was arrested on suspicion of the murder and lodged in the Long Ashton lock-up.

The inquest into the death of Mark Cox opened in the crowded schoolhouse at Ridgehill. The two surgeons gave evidence as to the cause and said that they had never seen a more shocking case of a fractured skull; great force must have been used to produce the massive injuries. The deceased's alleged fear of Job Wedlake was put in evidence and the coroner was informed that the young man was now in custody under suspicion of murder. Superintendent Drewett stated that enquiries were continuing and the inquest was adjourned for two days.

Suspicion had also fallen on Thomas Wedlake following allegations that Mark Cox had been frightened of him. A long waterproof coat belonging to his father was impounded by the police and found to be damp as if recently sponged and there were spots of blood on the right shoulder. The loan of the coat to a Winford butcher who confirmed that it had been worn when a calf was skinned, did not prevent Thomas being arrested on suspicion of murder; his statement that he had arrived home at about half past ten on the Sunday evening was also discounted. Both Job and Thomas Wedlake (they were cousins) were remanded in custody by the Long Ashton magistrates whilst the investigations continued.

Although there were two suspects in the lock-up at Long Ashton the case was far from complete. The evidence against the two Wedlakes was tenuous, both men's families swore that they were at home at the time it was believed the murder was committed, the murder weapon had not been found and although the blood stains on the coat had been analysed and found to be mammalian, in 1883 science could not tell whether they were human or animal. There also appeared to be no motive, the alleged threats appeared to be exaggerated and whatever the ill feeling no one could believe that it was deep enough to result in murder. Unless the police could provide sounder evidence it was unlikely that the magistrates would send the two men for trial on a capital charge.

Meanwhile Mark Cox had been buried in the churchyard at Chew Stoke and over seven hundred people attended the funeral which was paid for by the Redding Iron Ore Company who ran the Winford Iron Ore Works.

On the morning of Sunday 28 January the breakthrough came when Superintendent Drewett was informed that Thomas Wedlake, who had been very depressed for several days, wished to make a statement. He told the Superintendent that he did not see why he should be kept in prison for an offence which he had not committed while the guilty person went free. Superintendent Drewitt cautioned Thomas Wedlake and the prisoner made a written statement implicating his brother Joseph. He recounted the threats made against Alfred Thatcher on the night of the murder and suggested that Mark Cox had been killed by mistake. Thomas also mentioned the bulge at the back of his brother's coat which looked as if he had been concealing the weapon he had threatened to use on Alfred Thatcher.

Superintendent Drewett turned his dog-cart into the yard at the Pearce farm and Joseph Wedlake ran across to hold the horse as the policeman got out. The horse was unhitched and, after watching Joseph lead it into the stable, the Superintendent asked him to come into the house. There, in the presence of Farmer Pearce, the policeman told Joseph Wedlake that he was arresting him for the murder of Mark Cox. The young man made no reply but turned deathly pale and burst into tears.

Joseph wept all the way back to Long Ashton and remained silent when he was fully charged at the police station. The following day Superintendent Drewett returned to the farm and collected the hat and long coat believed to have been worn by the prisoner on the night of the murder. He searched the farm cellar and found the 'pig' axe which fitted Thomas Wedlake's description of the weapon.

On 30 January, Joseph Wedlake asked to speak to the Superintendent and told him that Job Wedlake had killed Mark Cox and anything his brother said about him was a lie. The policeman said that he had an urgent appointment and could not stop to take his statement in writing but as soon as he got back he would see the prisoner again. On his return, about four hours later, the Superintendent went down to Joseph Wedlake's cell and the prisoner, in tears, told him that Job Wedlake knew nothing about the murder. Now he would tell all about it.

Ordering the prisoner to follow him the policeman went to his office, produced pen and paper and, after being formally cautioned,

Joseph Wedlake began to make his statement in a faltering voice: 'I killed the man, sir; he was killed in mistake, sir. I killed him with a thing we got at home what uncle do kill the pigs with. That's the thing, sir [at which point the 'pig' axe was produced]. I was jealous of that young man Thatcher, and had a drop to drink. I am sorry now ever since I done it. I've had no sleep since, and should have been bound to split. I've had it on my mind ever since. I could not bear to go outside the door. Job Wedlake knew nothing about it. I done it myself. I keep on dreaming about it. I fancy I see him all the time. It was Horler that I met, and would not speak. It was a pity Horler did not catch hold of me. I should not have touched him. I cannot think how Horler did not know me.'

Joseph Wedlake completed his statement and, after it was read back to him by the Superintendent, he placed his mark on the document. However he had not finished baring his soul and Joseph went on to tell how he had met Mark Cox and wished him goodnight, how he had swung the axe and realised too late that it was Cox, and how he had struck two more blows when the victim was on the ground. Joseph Wedlake was brought before the Long Ashton magistrates and sent for trial at the next Assizes charged with the wilful murder of Mark Cox. Job and Thomas Wedlake were released.

The trial before Baron Huddleston began at ten-thirty on Monday morning 30 April 1883, the last day of the Spring Assizes in Taunton and Joseph Wedlake pleaded 'Not Guilty' to the indictment for the 'Wilful Murder of Mark Cox'. Mr Hooper and the Hon. Bernard Colleridge prosecuted and Mr Poole defended.

Mr Hooper opened for the Crown and recounted the events of the night of 7 January. He told the jury that the evidence he would place before them would disclose as strange a tale as they could hear. It would be a tale of honest, open love, of hidden passion and jealousy as cruel as the grave. They would see the congregation assembled in the village church and Thatcher walking home with his sweetheart and a friend, and they would hear the following footsteps of the layer-in-wait for blood. They would see Mark Cox leaving his fireside to go off to his labour on the night shift as soon the Sunday was passed and then, in the darkness and dead of night, they had the fearful tragedy, in which the poor lad was struck down by some blinding stroke of fate.

One by one the witnesses were called and recounted their actions on the night of the murder and during the following days. The medical men gave their testimony and confirmed that in their opinion the injuries had been caused by the 'pig' axe. Superintendent

Drewett outlined the investigations which had resulted in the arrest of Joseph Wedlake and testified to the accused's statement confessing his crime.

There were no witnesses for Joseph Wedlake but his counsel, Mr Poole, put up a spirited defence. He submitted that there was no evidence of hostility between the accused and Thatcher but there were others who might have had reason to commit the crime. Mr Poole questioned the testimony of Thomas Wedlake, the legality of the confession which his client had retracted, and counsel reminded the jury that it was not unknown for people to confess to crimes which they had not committed. In conclusion, Mr Poole submitted that on the evidence presented by the Crown, the jury could not find the case against the accused proved beyond reasonable doubt.

The judge, in summing up, told the jury that no feeling of sympathy or indignation must interfere with their returning a true and honest verdict, or make them shrink from the responsibility resting upon them. The question they had to consider was whether or not it was the prisoner's hand which had murdered Mark Cox. If he was mistaken in his victim it mattered not because it was still murder in the eyes of the law. The judge then reviewed the evidence and concluded by stating that if the jury believed that the prisoner had directed the blow which killed Mark Cox, their verdict must be one of Wilful Murder.

It was shortly after five o'clock in the afternoon when the jury retired to consider their verdict and a quarter of an hour later they returned and pronounced Joseph Wedlake 'Guilty'.

Addressing the prisoner, the judge stated that he had been convicted on the clearest evidence and by his own statement of the most cruel murder of Mark Cox. It was obvious that that the prisoner had not intended to kill the youth but it was plain that he was jealous and, motivated by hatred, was determined to remove Thatcher because of his favour for the young woman. The traditional black cap was placed on the judge's head and he passed sentence of death on Joseph Wedlake.

During that long April day Joseph Wedlake had been in a state of emotional collapse, sitting in the dock, trembling and crying with his head bowed and face hidden in his hands. Following the dreadful sentence he was led weeping down to the cells. The date of Joseph Wedlake's execution was fixed for 8 am on Monday 21 May, but he would not be alone on the scaffold in the County Gaol; George White, who had been convicted for killing his wife at Henstridge, had been sentenced to die on the same day.

During his final days Joseph was said to have been very penitent, frequently giving way to 'remorse and grief', and had expressed a preference for the extreme penalty rather than penal servitude for life. This preference, however, did not dissuade the Rector of Winford, the Reverend Henry Tripp, from making strenuous efforts to obtain a reprieve for Joseph Wedlake on the grounds of his having borne no ill will towards the youth whom he had killed by mistake, of his previously good character and of the remorse he had suffered since the crime. A petition for reprieve was presented to the Home Secretary but the promoters failed in their efforts to persuade Mr and Mrs Cox to join the appeal. The Home Secretary declined to advise Queen Victoria to commute the sentence to life imprisonment. Joseph Wedlake would hang.

On Saturday 19 May, as the scaffold was nearing completion, William Marwood, the official hangman and perfector of the long drop, arrived in Taunton. A few minutes before 8 am on Monday 21 May the bell of the County Gaol began to toll and the procession of officials, the Sheriff of Somerset and the two condemned men with their arms pinioned, slowly walked to the place of execution. Joseph Wedlake and George White were placed on the drop, their legs were strapped, white caps were pulled down over their faces and, at eight o'clock precisely, Marwood drew the bolt, the drop fell and both men died.

MRS ADLAM KILLS
HER HUSBAND

Mrs Mary Ada Adlam worked hard to make a living as a straw hat maker in Regency Bath, and her husband, Mr Henry Adlam, drank hard on the profits.

Wednesday, 18 May 1814, did not start well for Mrs Adlam at the shop in Bath Street because Mr Adlam was already on the way to his usual intoxicated state. When he was in this condition Mr Adlam was prone to violence and this day was to be no exception. The strong words between the husband and wife terminated when Mr Adlam, calling his wife a bitch and a whore, banged her head several times against the wall of the shop and stormed out to pursue another day's drinking in the city.

Mrs Adlam recovered, as usual, and with her new apprentice, Sarah Ellis, started work making and selling straw hats and bonnets for the benefit of Mr Adlam's passion for liquor.

Mrs Adlam and Sarah Ellis had just finished their tea in the small parlour next to the shop, when Mr Adlam returned, very intoxicated, and demanded his tea. Because Mrs Adlam wanted to use the parlour table for lining some bonnets, she asked her husband to have his tea downstairs in the kitchen and made to pick up the tray with the tea things and the remains of the meal of bread and butter.

Shouting that he'd be damned if he would not have some, Mr Adlam pulled his wife back by her gown, and swore that the tea things should not be removed. He rang the bell violently for the servant, Betty Whitehead, and when she appeared, told her to get some water for the pot.

Mrs Adlam picked up the tray but before she could hand it to Betty, Mr Adlam snatched it away and shouting that he would have his tea in the parlour, placed it on the side board and then punched his long suffering wife to the ground calling her a damned blasted whore. Painfully Mrs Adlam regained her feet only to be punched again and to hear her husband shouting at her to go back to London and her companions as she was a damned blasted whore!

Mr Adlam then reeled from the parlour and across the shop and fell down behind the counter. Distraught and in pain, Mrs Adlam followed, screaming for her husband to prove that she was a whore and if he believed so, why did he continue to live with her and let her support him. By now Mrs Adlam was in a great passion and, fearing that her mistress would be beaten again, Betty Whitehead grabbed her around the waist and prevented her from going further into the shop.

On his feet again, Mr Adlam contented himself for a few moments by sweeping material and hats from the counter onto the floor and began to advance across the shop swearing that he had not finished with his wife. From then on everything happened very quickly. Mrs Adlam stepped back into the parlour and immediately reappeared carrying the large case knife which had been used to cut the bread at tea-time. Waving the knife at her husband she dared him to repeat the accusations, which he did, calling her a damned blasted whore. For a moment a mixture of fear and fury burned in Mrs Adlam, then down slashed the knife cutting the left sleeve of her husband's jacket and she turned and rushed back into the parlour.

Looking down, Mr Adlam saw the cut and exclaimed to Sarah Ellis, 'She's cut me!' and as he stretched out his arm to show the young apprentice, blood poured from the sleeve. Horrified, Sarah cried out, 'Oh, Mr Adlam there is blood!' and called for her mistress.

Gently Mrs Adlam, all anger spent, took her husband's arm and managed to persuade the rapidly sobering and frightened man to go down to the kitchen. They managed two of the steep steps but then Mr Adlam stumbled and the couple crashed down the remaining 14 treads landing heavily on the stone flagged kitchen floor.

The injured man was hauled, fainting, by his wife and the servant onto a chair and Betty Whitehead tried unsuccessfully to stem the bleeding. Surgeon Day who lived nearby was soon in attendance and after bandaging the wound assured Mr Adlam that it was not serious; twenty-four hours later, thirty-year-old Mr Adlam was dead, and within another twenty-four hours, Mrs Adlam was in Ilchester Gaol, charged with the murder of her husband.

On 13 August 1814, Mrs Mary Ada Adlam was brought before the judge, Sir Vicary Gibbs, at the Somerset Assizes in Wells.

Sarah Ellis, the principal witness, stated that she had lived with Mr and Mrs Adlam for nine weeks before the fatal day, and had been learning the straw hat business. She had always found Mrs Adlam to be a 'tender humane woman' to her husband but he was often drunk and then he would be 'abusive and used the prisoner ill'. Sarah described the events of 18 May but although she had witnessed the beatings and the row at tea-time she did not see her mistress cut Mr Adlam because at that moment she had been picking up silver paper from the floor behind the counter. She testified that Mr Adlam had been very drunk at the time

Betty Whitehead, the Adlam's servant, stated that she had been in their employ for sixteen months and corroborated the evidence given by Sarah Ellis. She said that her master was often drunk and when in this state he was very abusive to his wife, calling her a whore and other things. Betty told the jury that during the row at tea-time on she had feared Mr Adlam would kill his wife. The witness recounted that just before Mr Adlam died she heard him tell his wife not to trouble herself because it was all his fault.

Elizabeth Figges, the third witness and a neighbour's servant, stated that she had been called to nurse Mr Adlam. At about nine o'clock on the following morning the patient had complained that his stomach hurt and of being in pain all over. Surgeon Goldstone was called and after examining Mr Adlam pronounced that he was dying.

The witness stated that during the time she had nursed the sick man he had repeatedly asked his wife not to grieve for him because it was his own fault and he begged her to stay by his side and kiss him time and time again.

In her written defence, which was read to the court, Mrs Adlam maintained her innocence and that 'from the abuse and provocation received from her husband, she was so irritated as not to be sensible of what she had done but concluded that in the height of her passion she must have given the fatal wound. She called upon God to witness the truth of her assertion and that she had no intention of doing him any harm.'

A number of witnesses now came forward to speak for Mrs Adlam. A former neighbour in Bath Street, Miss Elizabeth Gardner, stated that during the two years she had known the accused she had found her to be 'a very virtuous, humane, good sort of woman, very affectionate to her husband, and endeavouring to prevail on him to stay at home.' The witness had been present during the last few hours of Mr Adlam's life and recalled that the dying man had told her that he did not think his wife had deliberately cut him. Just before he died Mr Adlam had embraced his wife, kissed her and whispered, 'Mary, forgive me and make it up.'

Surgeons Day and Goldstone had attended Mr Adlam but at first neither thought the wound to be of much consequence and suggested that his death was partly caused by falling down the stairs, partly by excessive drinking and partly by passion.

The judge, Sir Vicary Gibbs, was not satisfied with this vague testimony and told the medical men that they must confine themselves to one question – did they think the wound caused the death? In reply the surgeons prevaricated suggesting that the wound was aggravated by the other circumstances.

The judge was still not satisfied and said that the question he had posed was a very plain one and he must have a direct answer. If the deceased had not been wounded with a knife, would the fall down the stairs, the inflamed state of his blood and the violent passion he was in, have caused his death? – Yes or No? The reply came, 'Certainly not!'

Sir Vicary Gibbs in his summing up for the jury read over the evidence and advised that language, no matter how foul and provoking, could not justify a person taking up a weapon and dealing a mortal blow to a fellow creature. But if they thought that the blow was struck whilst the quarrel between the prisoner and the deceased was high, the crime could be softened down to manslaughter. If, however, they thought there was a sufficient lapse of time whereby the prisoner could have recovered from the moment of passion, a verdict of wilful murder must be given.

The jury deliberated for a few minutes and returned a verdict of Guilty to Manslaughter and Mrs Adlam fainted. On her recovery the judge sentenced her to six months imprisonment and she fainted again.

The general register of the County Gaol at Ilchester records that Mrs Mary Ada Adlam was discharged from the 'Common Gaol' on 13 February 1815. She then disappears into the mist of time.

'IT SHALL BE A LIFE FOR A LIFE BEFORE I SLEEP'

William Cornish did not like Mark Sheppard and he had made it very clear that he would not allow him to marry his daughter Mary. During the summer of 1817 the rejected suitor had seethed with anger and on more than one occasion he had been heard to threaten to kill William Cornish, the shoemaker of Stoke Lane, or Stoke St Michael as the Mendip village is now known.

Thomas Green and William Cornish had spent a long tiring day on 29 August at Shepton Mallet market and the Waggon and Horses was a welcome sight as they tramped home to Stoke Lane but not such a welcome sight, as the two men entered, was Mark Sheppard sitting drinking with a friend called Hancock. It was, however, a pleasant evening, the beer was good and the past unpleasantness between Cornish and Sheppard seemed to have evaporated in the summer heat. Or had it? As the beer flowed, tongues loosened but when Hancock joked about Sheppard wanting Mary Cornish, the place erupted. Shouting and swearing the two men leapt to their feet and squared up ready to fight. Being a canny landlord and expecting trouble, Benjamin Cornish was ready when it happened, and quickly parted the antagonists before they could begin to trade blows.

With an uneasy peace restored, every one sat down and, pouring Sheppard a glass of beer, William Cornish told him soothingly that he meant him no ill will. The rest of the evening passed without further trouble and at about 10 pm the shoemaker, in company with Thomas Green and Mark Sheppard, left the inn for their homes in Stoke Lane.

As they approached the crossroads at Three Ashes, the quarrel broke out again and, shouting abuse at each other, Cornish and Sheppard began to grapple at the side of the road. Thomas Green managed to part them before any serious blows were struck but at the crossroads Sheppard started to shout and swear again. William Cornish, however, did not respond and kept walking down the road with Green. For a moment Sheppard stood shouting but instead of following, turned to his right and hurried up the lane which also led to the village.

Hester Cornish was becoming a little annoyed when midnight passed and husband William had still not returned from Shepton market. Although it was not like him to be so late coming home, she told herself that he had probably stopped off at Thomas Green's and gave him a little longer.

When William had not arrived by 1 am Hester became really worried and daughter Mary was sent down to Thomas Green's to find out where he was. Mary found her father lying in the road and her first thoughts were that he was drunk. Putting the lantern to his face she recoiled with horror and nausea, her father's head was a smashed, bloody mess and in the wavering light she glimpsed his eyes hanging from gory sockets and the glint of teeth in the dust of the road. Screaming, the young woman ran to Thomas Green's and banging on the door raised the household.

The body of William Cornish was taken home and an inquest held later in the day. Suspicion was centred immediately on Mark Sheppard because of the well-known ill-feeling between the two men and the disputes at the Waggon and Horses and on the way home. Several witnesses came forward to testify that Sheppard had threatened the life of the deceased and the circumstantial evidence pointed to his guilt. The 23 inquest jurymen unanimously returned a verdict of Wilful Murder against Sheppard and he was committed to Shepton Mallet Gaol to await trial.

The Somerset Lent Assizes opened in Taunton on Monday 30 March 1818 and Mark Sheppard was brought before Mr Justice Abbott indicted for the Wilful Murder of William Cornish.

Thomas Green, the first witness, recalled the events of the August evening and the struggle in the road. After he had parted the two men, the prisoner had invited William Cornish to go with him up the lane but the deceased had shouted back, 'What do you want I to go that way, you calf!' Sheppard had sworn and then ran out of sight up the lane. The witness stated that the two of them had continued on their way to Stoke Lane and reaching his house at about 11 pm he had bidden William Cornish goodnight and gone in to bed.

Benjamin Cornish, the landlord of the Waggon and Horses, described the dispute at the inn and said that he had overheard the prisoner muttering that he would commit a violence on William Cornish before he got home and that he would soon die as live.

Richard Brown, who had been drinking at the Waggon and Horses, remembered the disturbance and testified that he had overheard the prisoner cursing and swearing that 'It would be a life for a life before I sleep and it should be damned if it should not.' The witness had been alarmed at Sheppard's threats and had begged him to go home quietly. Brown stated that the prisoner had been drinking heavily all evening.

Mary Cornish now took the stand and stated that her father would often call in at Thomas Green's house on his way from Shepton Mallet market. On 29 August her father had not arrived home at his normal time and her mother, becoming concerned, had sent her at about 1 am to Thomas Green's to see if he was there. The young woman paused, sobbed, and then recalled the terrible discovery of her father's battered body lying in the road. Mary stated that when his clothes were searched by the constable it was found that he had 12 shillings in silver and some papers in his pockets.

The next witness was Mr Stratford, a resident of the small hamlet of Three Ashes, who testified that at about 11 pm on the night of the murder he had heard quarrelling in the road outside. Climbing out of bed he had looked out of his window and in the bright moonlight he could clearly see William Cornish standing on one side of the road and the prisoner on the other. He heard the deceased call Sheppard a 'calf' and in response the prisoner had shouted that there was no occasion to call him a 'calf' because he always paid what he owed. William Cornish had yelled that he might have paid his debts but only after a good looking after.

The witness then recalled that the prisoner had tauntingly invited the deceased to go up the lane with him but he heard William Cornish refuse and saw him hurry away down the road.

Mr Stratford stated that the prisoner shouted, 'Cornish, I'll be even with thee before morning' and then went off up the lane swearing and cursing.

The witness then related how, early in the following morning, he had found that a wooden rail had been torn from his garden gate.

Mary Ann Brown testified that at the time of the murder she lived in Mr Ryall's house at Three Ashes and, hearing the sound of the quarrel, had looked out and seen the prisoner walking away up the lane. Mr Ryall, who was married to the prisoner's sister, had been ill and the witness was his nurse. She recalled that some time between midnight and 1 a.m., Mark Sheppard had come to the house and said that he had been asleep in the lane and thought his sister's house was handier for him than to go home. The prisoner was tipsy and wanted to send for some beer for his brother-in-law, but when told it was too late, he had lain down in the parlour and gone to sleep. He had got up just after 5 a.m., wandered around for a few minutes and saying nothing lay down again until 6 am Mrs Ryall had gone out at about that time and shortly after, hurried back with the news that William Cornish had been killed and his brains beaten out. Mary Brown noticed that on hearing the report, Mark Sheppard had hung his head and said that he could not think William Cornish was dead, and if he was, it was done by some bad fellow who wanted to take his money. Shortly after, he drank two cups of tea and, in company with his sister, the prisoner had left.

James Green, who was married to one of the deceased's daughters, testified that at about 2 am he had been called to his father-in-law's house and found him dead. As soon as it was daylight he had been taken to the place where the body was found and, after a search, he had recovered a piece of wood covered with blood and brains, pushed into a nearby hedge. The length of wood was now shown to the witness who testified that it was the piece he had found near the place of the murder. Mr Stratford, recalled to the stand, testified that the wood compared with the piece removed from his gate.

The parish constable, Robert Rossiter, now produced the prisoner's coat and cravat which he had been wearing when taken into custody on the day of the inquest and showed the jury spots of blood on both garments.

Mary Diniman testified that some two or three months before the murder, the prisoner had been cursing William Cornish because he had heard that he did not wish his daughter to enter Sheppard's family and had vowed to kill Cornish.

During the enquiries into the murder some suspicion had fallen on the prisoner's brother, Edward Sheppard, and he was called to the witness box. Doubtless it was a rather apprehensive man who swore that he was in bed at home with the door locked before 11 pm on the night of 29 August. He stated that his brother had not come home at any time during the night and denied that he had told anyone that his brother came in and stayed for a few minutes. Edward Sheppard stated that the clothes his brother wore on the day he was arrested were the same as those he had gone out in on the night of the murder.

All the evidence had now been presented and the judge, Mr Justice Abbott, turned to the jury and began his summing up. He stated that without doubt there had been great animosity between the deceased and the prisoner for some while before the fatal day. The two men had been prevented on two occasions from fighting during that evening and this had been witnessed by a number of people. It was true that the prisoner had not confessed to the murder and no one had seen the commission of the crime, but the threats to kill Cornish on the evening of his death and the evidence of blood on the clothes the prisoner had worn on the night were important factors to be considered by the members of the jury when coming to their verdict.

However the members of the jury had already made up their minds and after a moment's consultation returned a verdict of 'Guilty.' The *Western Flying Post* reported that the prisoner behaved with shocking levity throughout his trial and appeared quite unconcerned when the dreadful sentence of the law was pronounced.

Mark Sheppard was taken to Ilchester Gaol where he was executed on Monday 13 April and his body handed over to the Medical Institution of Bridgwater for dissection. The chaplain of Ilchester Gaol, Thomas G. Rees, wrote in his notebook that, ' Mark Sheppard, age 23, was executed at Ilchester April 13, 1818, for the murder of William Cornish, shoemaker. He denied having committed the murder till within a few minutes of his death when he reluctantly confessed his guilt and said that he was not the only person concerned. From circumstances and what he hinted there was reason to suppose that his brother was concerned and implicated with him which was the occasion of his not making a more open and candid confession than he did. He refused taking the sacrament.'

High on the west wall inside the parish church of Stoke St Michael there is a memorial tablet which reads:

Sacred
To the memory of
WILLIAM CORNISH
who was Barbarously Murdered
on the 29th of August 1817
in the 51st Year of his Age
Leaving a disconsolate Widow and
Seven Children to deplore their loss
and his untimely end.

JACOB WILKINS GOES A-COURTING – FOR THE LAST TIME

Widower Jacob Wilkins was going a-courting resplendent in his Sunday best, his pockets full of half-crowns and proudly displaying his fine silver watch and chain. The fifty-year-old ostler of the Blucher Inn at Norton St Philip set out on foot from his cottage at half past eleven on Sunday morning, 1 August 1824, to pay his addresses to Mrs Mary Lovington, widow of Bath, whom he hoped to marry.

At about 2 pm he arrived at his lady friend's house in the city where he enjoyed a leisurely luncheon and a pleasant afternoon in her company. In the early evening the couple, accompanied by two female acquaintances, walked to the Cross Keys Inn where they all drank some beer. At about 8 pm they parted and Jacob Wilkins set off on the road home to Norton St Philip.

As the ostler walked down the hill towards the Fox Inn at Midford he noticed a ruddy-faced young man leaning against a gate who called out a greeting as he passed. Following an exchange of pleasantries and, hearing that he was walking to Norton St Philip, the young man joined Jacob Wilkins saying that he would accompany him so far as Hinton Charterhouse. Arriving outside the Fox Inn, his companion suggested that they go in for a jug of beer but the invitation was declined by the ostler who said that he had no money and so they walked on past and began to climb Midford Hill.

Later that evening at about half past nine Samuel Huntley and two young ladies left the Fox Inn and had walked about half a mile up Midford Hill towards Hinton Charterhouse when a young man, wearing a dark waistcoat and light breeches, came hurrying down towards them. As he passed he called out that there was a man lying drunk in the road and he had been two hours trying to get him on his feet. Samuel Huntley and his two companions continued on their way and as they rounded a bend a few hundred yards further along they saw the man lying in the dust. It took only a cursory glance to tell them that this was not a drunk but a corpse, with its pockets turned out and a badly bruised face. Telling his two friends to get help, Samuel ran back down the hill after the young man but he had disappeared.

The body was taken to the Fox Inn where it was confirmed that the dead man had been beaten and robbed and was identified as Jacob Wilkins, the ostler of the Blucher Inn.

At about 10 pm there was a hammering on the door of the Red Lion Inn at Odd Down, near Bath, and when she opened it, Ann Fisher, the landlord's servant, was confronted by a distressed young man soaked in sweat, wearing a dark waistcoat and light breeches and who asked for a jug of beer. The inn being closed Ann Fisher refused but the young man pleaded that he felt sick and very fatigued as he had been walking all day from Weymouth. Seeing how hot and tired he looked, the servant relented and, inviting him to take a seat, brought a jug of beer which he consumed with relish. Now refreshed, the young man asked for a candle to be lit and in the wavering light Ann Fisher looked on as he tried to wind a fine silver watch. She also observed that when the bill was paid he had on him a large amount of silver coin.

It did not take long for the brutal murder and robbery of Jacob Wilkins to be on everyone's lips between Bath and Norton St Philip and the search was on for a young man dressed in a dark waistcoat and light breeches. The suspect was soon identified as James Reynolds, an eighteen-year-old petty thief who had recently been released from the County Gaol after serving a twelve month sentence for robbery; he had also narrowly missed being convicted on a capital charge of horse-stealing due to lack of evidence.

Early on the Monday morning a young man arrived in the village of South Stoke near Bath and offered a silver watch to be raffled. However there were insufficient takers and finally he sold the watch to Samuel Noele, the ostler at the Stoke Inn, for 16 shillings.

Mr George Fisher, a farmer of South Stoke, was told of the sale and having heard of the murder and robbery of Joseph Wilkins he became suspicious. The farmer's enquiries soon confirmed his suspicions and, with the assistance of some of his labourers, the young man was seized as he sat outside the village inn. Despite his protestations of innocence he was brought before Mr Edmund Anderdon, the local magistrate, and named as James Reynolds, who also went under the alias of James Walters. The watch he had sold to Samuel Noele was identified as having belonged to Joseph Wilkins, but Reynolds swore that he had bought it for £1 from a stranger he had met on the road from Bath. He refused, however, to account for his movements the night before.

The magistrate spent the rest of Monday examining witnesses and the following morning James Reynolds was committed to Ilchester Gaol to await trial at the forthcoming Assizes. A verdict of Wilful Murder was returned against Reynolds by the jury at the inquest into Jacob Wilkins' death.

The trial of James Reynolds, alias Walters, for the Wilful Murder of Jacob Wilkins and the stealing of a silver watch with the value of 20 shillings, was held before Sir Charles Abbott at Somerset Summer Assizes in Wells on 28 August and long before the court opened at 9 a.m., the streets were thronged with people anxious for a glimpse of the prisoner.

Mr Gunning, counsel for the prosecution, outlined the case against the accused and described the events leading to his arrest.

His first witness was George Wilkins, son of the deceased, who confirmed that when his father had left home he had been wearing the silver watch sold by the prisoner. Mrs Mary Lovington described the last afternoon she had spent with Jacob Wilkins and testified that he was wearing the silver watch when he had bidden her good evening at the Cross Keys Inn. Samuel Huntley recalled finding the body and identified James Reynolds as the young man he had met on Midford Hill.

John Wheeler testified that the prisoner had left the Fox Inn at 7 pm on the Sunday evening and gone towards Bath but he had returned along the road between 8 pm and 9 pm in company with the deceased. The witness had overheard Jacob Wilkins decline the prisoner's invitation to have some beer saying that he had no money and remembered Reynolds saying, 'Well then we will go to Hinton.'

Ann Fisher, the servant at the Red Lion Inn recognised the prisoner as the young man who had called on the Sunday night and identified the silver watch he had tried to wind as that owned by the deceased.

William Perry stated that the prisoner had returned to the lodgings they shared at Burnt Hill at about 11 pm on the Sunday night in an agitated condition. He had shown the witness a silver watch and some money, but would not say how he had come by the articles. Early the following morning the prisoner had left saying that he was going to Bath. The witness had never known Reynolds to have a watch before.

Samuel Noele testified that he had bought the silver watch from James Reynolds for 16 shillings at South Stoke on 2 August. On hearing of the murder and robbery and Mr Fisher's enquiries he had taken the watch to the farmer.

At this moment Mr George Fisher was asked to produce the watch and the witnesses formally identified it as either belonging to the deceased or seen in the possession of the prisoner.

Mr George Goldstone, surgeon of Bath, stated that death had been caused by a violent blow to the left side of the head which had fractured the skull. He believed that a round stick had been used to inflict the injury. The parish constable was called and testified that when the prisoner had been in his custody he had said that no one had seen him do the deed and therefore they could not hang him for having Jacob Wilkins' watch. Before the witness could continue, the prisoner, who until now had shown little emotion or interest in the proceedings, shouted out, 'That's false, my Lord!' but the constable insisted that he was telling the truth.

The prosecution's case was now complete and Reynolds was called upon for his defence. Protesting his innocence he swore that he had bought the silver watch from a man called Lacy but then said no more. The judge, Sir Charles Abbott, summed up the evidence for the jury who took ten minutes to find James Reynolds guilty of the Wilful Murder of Jacob Wilkins and he was sentenced to be hanged.

The condemned man was taken to Ilchester Gaol to await his execution and there he confessed. He stated that he had met Jacob Wilkins between the Cross Keys and the Fox Inn at Midford and seeing the watch chain he became determined to steal it. Having got into conversation with the deceased he had walked with him towards Hinton Charterhouse and going up the Midford Hill he had picked up a stone about the size of a hen's egg. He had concealed it in his hand and about half way up the hill had struck Jacob Wilkins one blow on the side of his head. The man had fallen down on his face and he had taken the silver watch and some coins. Reynolds expressed his great sorrow and said that he had only meant to stun Jacob Wilkins.

At 11 am on Monday 6 September before a small crowd of onlookers, a weeping James Reynolds was launched into eternity on the scaffold in front of Ilchester Gaol. His body was conveyed that afternoon to Mr Lyddon, surgeon of Taunton, for dissection.

WHO CUT THE ROPE? – THE RADSTOCK PIT DISASTER

Four o'clock on a November morning can be a daunting time to begin the day's toil. But then to be lowered on the end of a rope hundreds of feet down a narrow shaft into the black bowels of the earth must be more so, even if you have done it as a means of earning a meagre living for years. But this was the daily round for miners working in the Somerset coalfields during the early years of the nineteenth century.

The morning shift had assembled at 4 am on Friday 8 November 1839 at the Wells Way Coal Pit, sunk some ten years before at Radstock, and was preparing to spend another back-breaking eight hours toiling deep under the Somerset hills.

There was Richard Langford, at forty-four the oldest of the 12 men and boys, with his two sons, sixteen-year-old Farnham and Alfred, thirteen; forty-one-year-old James Keevil and his lads, Mark and James, fifteen and fourteen; John Barnett, forty-one; William Summers, twenty-six; William Adams, nineteen; James Pearce, eighteen; Amos Dando, thirteen; and twelve-year-old Leonard Dowling.

The miners climbed on to the winding-rope and sitting in the hooked on loops, the youths hanging on individually and the boys in the laps of the men, they waited for the loading planks to be removed from the mouth of the round 4 feet 6 inch shaft and to start their journey down to the pit 756 feet below.

The signal was given to lower away, the steam engine hissed, machinery began to rumble as the brakes were released on the winding drum, the loading planks were pulled back, the rope took the weight and William Summers the man hooked on at the top screamed, 'What's the matter with the rope – how it jumps!'

For a moment there was silence, even the noise of the machinery and steam seemed to be in suspense, then came a wailing shriek from the shaft, a crash from the roof of the shed as the rope flew over the top of the winding-wheel and followed the 12 men and boys down into the black hole.

At the entrance to the bottom of the shaft the seven men of the Thursday night shift waited patiently for their relief, there was little conversation, they were too tired and just wanted to get home. The shrieks sounded as if the doors of hell had been opened, seven pairs of eyes flashed white in blackened faces in the flickering candle light, there was a rush of air followed by a squelching, cracking thud, the like of which the seven would never forget. It was the sound that 12 men and boys make after falling 756 feet down a 4 feet 6 inch shaft.

Within minutes loops had been hooked on to the winding-rope and three brave men were lowered down the shaft and in the feeble light of their candles they found a sickening pile of bodies, smashed beyond recognition in an horrific steaming, bloody mess. They also found seven hardened Somerset miners shocked speechless by the terrible sight they had just witnessed.

The news of the disaster quickly drew fellow miners and the families of the four o'clock shift to the coal works and there were heart-rending scenes of distress as parents, wives and children milled around the pit head.

Soon there was rumour of something not quite right with the breaking of the rope and then there were cries of 'Murder' as the broken ends were inspected. The flat rope, five inches wide and one and a quarter inches thick, was made from four interwoven hemp cables and close examination revealed that where it had given way, there were signs that the rope had been deliberately weakened, possibly by being placed on a stone and struck with a crowbar or pick. The ends of the outside fibres were seen to be fairly even and level as if cut whereas those inside were torn, jagged and uneven.

The Somerset coroner, Mr R. Uphill, did not delay matters and later that Friday he opened the inquest into the deaths of the 12 men and boys.

The first witness was George Kingston, manager of the Radstock Wells Way Coal Pit, who stated that the winding rope was less than six months old and during this time had regularly worked with weights of up to $2^1/_2$ tons. The night before seven men had gone down the shaft and the rope was perfectly secure.

The witness stated that he was at the pit early that morning and saw the 12 men and boys hooked on and ready to go down, when suddenly the rope broke and the end came over the wheel striking the roof of the shed in which he was standing. Another rope was made ready and he had sent Thomas Hill and two other men down the pit to see what could be done. On their return, they had told him that all the twelve had been dashed to pieces at the bottom.

After the Thursday night shift had gone down everything appeared to be in order and as he left the pit head at about 8.15 pm there was no one about. The witness went on to say that he had slept at the works all night and had heard no noise.

The manager stated that in his opinion the rope had been deliberately weakened by some person or persons so that it would break. In conclusion George Kingston said that he knew of no ill feeling among the men and he had always believed they were on the most friendly terms.

Thomas James, the next witness, stated that he was at the mouth of the shaft and when the 12 men and boys were ready to be lowered he began to pull back the loading planks. At that moment William Summers, the top man, shouted out that there was something the matter with the rope but the witness had called back that he could see nothing wrong and uncovered the mouth of the shaft; immediately the men had fallen to the bottom of the pit. James stated that he had been shown the severed rope and he considered that it had been wilfully and maliciously injured.

The third witness, John Fricker, corroborated Thomas James' evidence and shared his opinion on the malicious injury to the winding rope.

George Short testified that he cleaned and helped to load the coal at the pit. He had left his pick and shovel buried under a pile of coal at the mouth of the pit when he had finished work the previous evening and on returning this morning he had found the implements undisturbed.

Thomas Hill stated that with two fellow miners he had gone down the pit after the fall and had found all 12 dead in a mass of steaming human gore. He testified that the rope was quite sound at 8 pm the previous evening when the night shift had gone down.

Having heard the witnesses, the jury, after a short consultation returned a verdict of 'Wilful Murder against some person or persons unknown.'

News of the jury's verdict spread rapidly across the Somerset coalfield and emotions were running high. Work in the pits was hard and dangerous with risks enough, but the thought of the malicious damage to the miners' life line was almost too much to bear in the closely knit mining communities. If the culprit or culprits were found they would be in great danger of being summarily strung up or thrown down the nearest coal pit.

At the close of the inquest the proprietors of the Wells Way Works gave orders for a suitable coffin to be provided for each body but because they could not be individually identified, the names of the victims could not be placed on the lids. The mass funeral took place on the following Sunday afternoon when, to the sound of tolling bells and in pouring rain under a grey sky, the 12 coffins, each carried by four miners, made their sombre way from the Wells Way pit to the parish church of Midsomer Norton. Over 4000 people followed to the churchyard gate where the procession was met by the Reverend C.O. Mayne and led into the church. After reading a portion of Scripture, the Rev. Mr Mayne addressed the mourners and called their attention to the affecting scene which then presented itself. The *Taunton Courier* recorded that the Reverend Gentleman went on to say 'that he hoped they would receive his observations as from that God whom he trusted they all served. It has not, said Mr Mayne, ever fallen to my lot, nor, perhaps, to any other minister of God, to witness such an awful scene as the one before us; twelve of our brethren consigned to an early and unexpected tomb! In gazing on it, we as mortals may be tempted to say, God has dealt harshly with us; but when we consider the iniquity which prevails, even in our parish; the scenes of Sabbath-breaking, immorality, drunkeness, swearing, adultery, and other vices, let us ask, is it not a slight visitation compared with our deserts? The Reverend speaker then most affectionately appealed to the miners generally and exhorted them to a reformation of their lives; and further observed, while we thus mourn we should be comforted by the recollection of the fact that some of these our brethren, had they been spared a few minutes longer, would have approached a throne of heavenly grace; but God called them from us, to appear before his throne in glory. Mr Mayne concluded his solemn address with words of spiritual consolation and comfort to the bereaved.'

The 12 coffins were then borne to their grave by the west wall of the churchyard in which they were placed four abreast. One of the distraught widows was heard to cry out as the coffins passed, 'One! Two! Three! Four! there, perhaps that's mine', and then collapsed in a frenzy of despair.

The disaster had left three widows, 12 young children fatherless and nine couples to mourn their sons. An appeal for the widows was launched and £25. 6s. 2¹/₂d. was quickly collected from Radstock alone.

To prevent another calamity, instructions were given to send down a fully-laden coal bucket before the miners descended into the pit and various suggestions were made to improve the safety of the men as they were lowered. An Admiral Bullen suggested that instead of one rope there should be two of equal size and strength. One, the working rope used by the men to ascend and descend, and the other, the safety rope which would have a large strong net-bag attached which would envelop the men as they sat on the hooks suspended by the working rope. Should the working rope break 'the men would be received into the net and saved from being precipitated down the shaft.'

Despite the offer by the Coal Masters of a reward of £100 for the apprehension of the perpetrator of the outrage, no one was ever arrested and neither was the reason established for the killing. There was, however, the suggestion of a personal grudge against one of the men, and another that someone had sought to kill the manager who often went down the pit alone on the rope.

From this distance in time it is unlikely that we will ever know whether the tragedy at 4 am on the morning of 8 November 1839 was a deliberate act of terrible malice, or perhaps, the result of negligence covered up, or maybe a pure accident. Whatever the cause, these men and boys died needlessly under the green hills of Somerset.

To remind future generations of the toll the mines could take, there is a gravestone against the west wall of Midsomer Norton churchyard bearing the words:

In this grave are deposited the remains of the twelve under-mentioned sufferers all of whom were killed at Wells Way Coal works on 8th November 1839 by snapping of the rope as they were on the point of descending into the pit. The rope was generally believed to have been maliciously cut.

THE SHOOTING OF
JOHN DYER AT THE BELL

Robert Johnson, the driver of the Bristol Mail Coach met up with fellow coachman, Bill Guion, during the late afternoon of Thursday, 22 December, in the year of 1808, and they decided upon an evening's drinking. They made their way through Bath to Stall Street and The Bell public house kept by Widow Roy, the mother of James Taylor, a friend of Bill Guion.

As they sipped their first glass of beer in the tap room, another of James Taylor's many friends, coachman John Dyer, came in out of the winter's evening and after ordering supper the three men adjourned to the parlour where a cheery fire had been made up for them.

David Rice, a tailor of Avon Street, and a lady friend arrived at The Bell sometime after eight o'clock and the coachmen invited the couple to join them in the parlour.

At about the same time James Taylor came home to the public house, and joined the customers in front of the cheerful parlour fire. Twenty two years old, James, was the only son of Widow Roy by her first husband and although a generally good natured and friendly young man, he was spoilt and could develop a violent temper when in liquor. He had shown little aptitude or interest in business drifting from job to job and spending more time in the city's public houses with 'idle friends'. However, James had married Rebecca Rudman a few months before and as she was now in the family way, Widow Roy was no doubt hoping that her wayward son would settle down.

When James Taylor joined the party before the parlour fire all the pieces had been put in place for the tragedy which would now begin to move inexorably to its climax four months later at the Stone Gallows outside Taunton.

After supper, the party was entertained by James Taylor demonstrating how he could bite flat a silver spoon and then coins were tossed for rounds of drinks. The parlour became noisier as the beer flowed and the stakes were enlarged to tossing for silver shillings and then for golden guineas.

When David Rice won a guinea from Robert Johnson they agreed to call for a second guinea with John Dyer acting as stake-holder. Rice won again, but this time Johnson called unfair. Although Rice did not agree, he wanted no trouble and so the two men tossed but Rice won once again. He then asked Dyer to hand over the winnings but Johnson called unfair throw and Dyer refused to pay out. Turning to James Taylor, the exasperated David Rice asked him to decide who had won, and favouring Rice, Taylor told the loser to pay up, but once again Johnson refused.

The steady consumption of alcohol now turned, what to sober men would have been and argument, into an explosive situation.

Johnson shouted that the money had not been fairly won and when he called Taylor a liar, the young man leapt to his feet and picking up his chair threw it across the parlour challenging anyone to fight him. When his invitation was declined Taylor stripped off his jacket and waistcoat and swept some glasses from the supper table.

With arms flailing he went for Johnson, wrestling him out of the parlour into the passage and they tumbled headlong down the stairs into the cellar. The fall calmed both men but when they returned to the parlour Johnson discovered that a brooch he wore had disappeared and demanded that it be found.

Apologising for his behaviour, Taylor suggested that they all have another drink, and offered to replace the brooch if he could not find it in the morning. However, Johnson refused the offer, saying that the brooch had his name on it and he would have it found now. Taylor consented and in company with Bill Guion, went back down into the cellar. The brooch was quickly recovered but as the two men climbed the stairs, Guion began to berate Taylor for fighting. Back in the parlour tempers once again boiled over and Taylor and Guion traded blows. As the two men fought each other into the passage, Widow Roy managed to pull them apart, but by now Taylor's shirt had been torn off and in a blind rage he ran up the stairs to his room; Guion ran into the tap room shouting for the poker.

Widow Roy followed her son up to his room and pleaded with him to stay there until he calmed down and she could get the coachmen to leave before there was more trouble. Fuelled by alcohol, Taylor was now beyond reason and his mother realising that the only solution was to clear the public house, ran back down the stairs to the tap room where she was confronted by a furious Bill Guion who hit her with the heavy iron poker he had taken from the fireplace.

As James Taylor stormed about his room he heard his mother screaming 'Murder, Murder', and throwing up the lid of his trunk, he took out a pair of primed and loaded pistols.

Charging down the stairs with a pistol in each hand, Taylor burst into the tap room where he saw his mother cowering on the settle and

Guion standing over her brandishing the heavy poker.

Fearing for his mother's safety, the son reacted instinctively and fired. The heavy lead pistol ball smashed into Guion's face and yelling 'I'm a dead man!', he crashed to the floor.

Moments later James Taylor, partly blinded by the muzzle flash and smoke and deafened by the concussion, sensed a threat from behind and spinning round he glimpsed a dark figure and fired his second pistol.

Watchman, William Roberts, was on duty in Stall Street and had just called 'Past one o'clock' when he heard the sounds of a disturbance coming from The Bell Public House. At first he took little notice but when he heard the cries of 'Murder' he ran across and sprung his rattle to summon assistance. The watchman hammered on the door which was opened by a terrified servant girl who fled into the street. As he entered the dim passage, he saw a figure leap down the stairs and disappear into the tap room from which the shouts of 'Murder' were coming. Just as Roberts reached the tap room door a man, whom he recognised as John Dyer, came out of the parlour but as the watchman pushed past him there was a brilliant flash followed by a deafening bang. Peering into the tap room, Roberts saw the naked back of a man who suddenly turned and for a moment to his horror, he was looking down the black muzzle of a pistol which exploded in a yellow flash.

The heavy lead ball missed William Roberts by a fraction but did not miss John Dyer who was standing behind him. The ball tore into his throat just under the point of the chin, passed down the left side of the neck, ripped the trachea, severed the carotid artery and hitting the bones of the neck was deflected out of John Dyer through the top of his left shoulder; within moments he was dead.

In his blind rage, Taylor began to beat the stunned watchman with his empty pistol and rained blow after blow on the poor man's head until the butt broke in half. Casting round for another weapon to continue with the beating, Taylor found the iron poker but before he could inflict further injury on the unfortunate Roberts, two watchmen summoned by the sound of the rattle and the pistol shots rushed in and disarmed him.

James Taylor was taken under guard to the watch house and Surgeon George Norman summoned to treat the casualties. John Dyer was dead lying in a pool of blood in the passage, Bill Guion lay on the settle in the tap room bleeding from a serious gun shot wound in his face and William Roberts, the watchman was suffering from a severe beating.

Shortly after he was lodged in the watch house, James Taylor passed out and could remember nothing from the time he had heard his mother's cries of 'Murder' until he came round later in the morning. He was horrified to be told that he had shot two men and was mortified when told that he had killed his friend John Dyer and seriously wounded Bill Guion. It was all a ghastly nightmare but one from which he could not awake.

The Inquest Jury returned a verdict of 'The Wilful Murder of John Dyer' against James Taylor and he was committed for trial at the Assizes.

A truly penitent James Taylor appeared before Baron Thompson at the Somerset Lent Assizes in Taunton on Friday 7 April, 1809. During his imprisonment he had shown overwhelming remorse for shooting his friend and it was not without difficulty that he was persuaded to plead not guilty to the indictment. Despite the efforts of his counsel in pleading provocation and self defence, the Jury found the accused guilty and he was sentenced to be executed on the coming Monday.

At about half past eight on Monday morning, 10 April, James Taylor climbed into the cart which would convey him to the Stone Gallows, some 2 miles outside Taunton. The route was lined with spectators and it was reported that seeing some of them weeping James Taylor had leaned from the cart and told them not to mourn for him but to have regard for their own souls.

Arriving at the fatal spot, the cart was positioned under the gallows and James Taylor's last moments were recorded by a friend:

The Chaplain then went up into the cart to him and delivered an address and a suitable form of prayer, at the conclusion of which he quitted the cart, leaving the prisoner still upon his knees. He continued his private devotions for eight or ten minutes. He then rose up and looked earnestly around him, evidently in search of some Christian friends, who had promised to accompany him to the place of suffering, and whose carriage was near the gallows. On their shewing themselves to him and catching his eye, he raised his hands and eyes to heaven with a look which clearly manifested and was designed to indicate to them that he still experienced the same gracious support which had been hitherto so bountifully imparted to him. He now yielded his hands and neck to the executioner, and assisted him in the performance of his office. On the usual signal being given by the prisoner by dropping a handkerchief, the cart was drawn away, and he was left suspended. A circumstance now occurred which has left an indelible impression on the memories of several persons who were present. After a lapse of some minutes he raised his hands which had been hanging down, and crossed them in a manner which he had been accustomed to adopt when he was engaged in devotional exercises thus proving what was the state of his soul to the last moment of his recollection. After this, with a slight convulsive motion, but without the least apparent agony or distortion he expired amidst the tears and lamentations of the surrounding multitude.

POSTSCRIPT

On 13 August, 1809, James, the son of James and Rebecca Taylor was baptised in St James's Church, Bath.

APPENDIX

THE LETTER FROM MR JUSTICE GASELEE
TO THE HOME SECRETARY

Montague Place 10th May 1830

Sir Before I received the Petition from Mr Erle in Favor of John Russell who was convicted before me at the last Assizes for the County of Somerset of Murder which you directed to be transmitted for my consideration Mr Hobhouse and Mr Phelips & Mr Coombe two other Magistrates of the County of Somerset had at my Request kindly undertaken to proceed to Chard to make Inquiry into several Particulars relative to the Case which appeared to require Investigation.

They have done so and upon their Report and a full consideration of all the Circumstances it appears to me to be advisable that the Convict should not be executed but should be transported for Life.

I have therefore to request that you will be pleased to make an application to His Majesty humbly praying him to grant to the Prisoner who is now in Ilchester Gaol and whose Execution has been respited until His Majestys Pleasure shall be known his most gracious Pardon on Condition of being Transported.

As soon as I received the Petition I transmitted it to Mr Hobhouse but it did not reach him until on his Return from Chard Mr Erle had however previously delivered to that Gentleman a statement containing the Substance of the Facts alledged in such Petition and the Accounts given by the several Persons to whom he referred in support of such Allegations and I had left with him the Notes of the Evidence of the Trial the Depositions before the Magistrates and Coroner with various other Papers which I had received.

I cannot close my letter without expressing my sense of the Obligation which I feel myself under and I think the County is so too, to Mr Hobhouse Mr Phelips and Mr Combe for the great Trouble and Pains which they have taken upon this occasion. I return you Mr Erle's Petition and have the Honor to be

> Your most faithful
> and obedient servant
> S Gaselee

On the back of the third sheet is written: 'John Russell. To be Transported for Life, May 11 1830.

SOURCES

KILLED FOR A PIECE OF BACON
Western Gazette, 20 & 27 March, 24 April 1874
J.W.Sweet, *Somerset Magazine*, April 1993

'NOTHING HAS EVER BEEN ADMINISTERED TO HER IN HER
  FOOD'
Western Flying Post, 10 & 31 July 1860
J.W.Sweet, *Somerset Magazine*, June 1995

THE DEVIL OF DEAD MAN'S POST
Western Flying Post, 3 May, 23 August 1830

THE UNTIMELY END OF CONSTABLE PENNY
Western Flying Post, 28 January, 1 April 1862.
J.W.Sweet, *The Visitor*, January 1990.

THE KILLING OF DANDY JOE
Western Flying Post, 19 August 1843
J.W.Sweet, *Somerset Magazine*, January 1996

WHO KILLED MR STUCKEY?
Taunton Courier, 18 & 25 August, 2 & 15 September 1830
Western Flying Post, 16 & 30 August, 6 September 1830
Benjamin Hebditch Diary, Mrs K. Lewis and Ms E.M. Hebditch

'HOW YOUR HAND DO SHAKE, GEORGE.'
Western Gazette, 6 & 13 April, 25 May 1883
Letter from Rev. Mr Ainslie to the Home Secretary, Public Record
  Office, HO/144/117

'YE THOUGHTLESS YOUTHS A WARNING TAKE'
Western Flying Post, 23 December 1854, 3 April 1855
J.W.Sweet, *Somerset Magazine*, January 1997

'WHAT A FOOL I'VE BEEN – I'VE NOT DONE IT YET'
Western Gazette, 6 & 13 April 1883

THE KILLING IN THE CLOVER FIELD
Taunton Courier, 4 April 1839
Western Flying Post, 29 October 1838, 15 April 1839
Somerset County Gazette, 6 April 1839

THE SLAYING ON SANDPIT HILL
Taunton Courier, 11, 18 & 25 March, 8 April 1835
Western Flying Post, 6 & 13 April, 18 May 1835

SUFFER THE LITTLE CHILDREN
Western Gazette, 25 September, 2, 9 & 23 October, 6, 13 & 25
   November, 18 & 25 December 1874, 22 & 29 January, 5 February, 2,
   23 & 30 April, 29 October 1875
Pulmans Weekly News, 6 & 13 October 1874
Yeovil Cemetery Register 1875, Numbers 1887 & 1888

WHEN DEATH RODE THE SKIMMINGTON
Western Gazette, 21 April, 11 August 1871
Shepton Mallet Journal, 21 April, 11 August 1871
Wells Journal, 10 August 1871
Bridport News, November 1884
Roberts, *History of Lyme Regis*, 1834

THE FIGHT AT THE RUNNING HORSE
Western Flying Post, 15 April 1843
Somerset County Gazette, 19 August 1843

THE EXTRAORDINARY CASE OF INFANTICIDE AT CREWK-ERNE
Taunton Courier, 26 June 1843
Western Flying Post, 17 June, 19 August 1843
Somerset County Gazette, 27 May, 24 June, 19 August 1843

WHO CRUELLY MURDERED BETTY TRUMP?
Western Flying Post, 3 & 24 March, 7 April 1823
Sherborne Journal, 24 April, 1823, 25 August 1835
Dorset Chronicle, 17 September, 1835
William Flood, *Murder on Buckland Hill – Statement of Facts*
Respecting the Murder of Elizabeth Trump (1823), Somerset
   Archaeological and Natural History Society

'I AM FREE AND INNOCENT OF THE CRIME'
Taunton Courier, 9 & 23 December 1829, 14 & 21 April 1830, 15 May,
   23 June 1830
Sherborne Journal, 31 December 1829, 15 & 22 April 1830
Bath Journal, 7 December 1929
The Times, 7, 8, 10 & 12 April 1830
Arthur Hull's Diary Part 1, 1826 to 1844, Somerset Record Office,
   DD/CHG36
Chard History Group, *Chard in 1851*, No 5, 12-13
Petition of John Russell, 10 May 1830, PRO, HO17/103/No T08

'THAT FISHER'S MAD!'
Western Flying Post, 8 June, 17 August, 7 September 1844

THE WITHYPOOL POISONER
Taunton Courier, 15 July, 2 September 1829

THE MALIGNANT SHOOTING OF JOSEPH DUNFORD
Dorset Chronicle, 11 May, 20 August 1835

A JEALOUSY AS CRUEL AS THE GRAVE
Wells Journal, 11 January, 1 February 1883
Taunton Courier, 17, 24 & 31 January, 14 February 1883
Somerset County Herald, 8 February, 26 May 1883
Western Gazette, 26 May 1883
Bristol Times, 1 May 1883

MRS ADLAM KILLS HER HUSBAND
Bath Chronicle, 22 August 1814
Taunton Courier, 25 August 1814

'IT SHALL BE A LIFE FOR A LIFE BEFORE I SLEEP'
Western Flying Post, 8 September 1817, 13 April 1818

JACOB WILKINS GOES A-COURTING – FOR THE LAST TIME
Bath Chronicle, 9 August, 1 September 1824
Bath & Cheltenham Gazette, 6 September 1824
Western Flying Post, 6 & 13 September 1824

WHO CUT THE ROPE? – THE RADSTOCK PIT DISASTER
Taunton Courier, 13 & 20 November 1839

Somerset County Gazette, 16 & 30 November 1839
Bath Chronicle, 14 November 1839
Bath & Cheltenham Gazette, 12 & 19 November 1839
Fred Flower, *Somerset Coal Mining Life – A Miner's Memories*, Millstream Books, Bath, 1990
C.G. Down and A.J. Warrington, *The History of the Somerset Coal Fields*, David and Charles, Newton Abbot, 1971

THE SHOOTING OF JOHN DYER AT THE BELL
Western Flying Post, 26 December, 1808, 17 April 1809
Bath Journal, 17 April 1809
Divine Mercy Exemplified in the Case of James Taylor who was Executed at Taunton on the Tenth of April 1809 for the Murder of John Dyer. Somerset Studies Library, Ref. 0086209